PAINLESS PERFECT GRAMMAR:

The National Grammar Hotline's Most Frequently Asked Questions

by **Michael Strumpf,**
founder of the National Grammar Hotline
with **Auriel Douglas**

BANDANNA BOOKS

Bandanna Books, 319-B Anacapa St., Santa Barbara CA 93101.
(805)962-9915 • FAX (805) 564-3278
Email: bandanna@west.net

http://www.west.net./~bandanna

ISBN 0-942208-43-9   LC applied for

"The question is," said Alice, *"whether you can make words mean so many different things."*

"The question is," said Humpty Dumpty, *"which is to be master—that's all."*

Lewis Carroll
Through the Looking Glass

Contents

This book is dedicated to all those with a sincere desire to learn, who have not called the National Grammar Hotline because they didn't know it existed, or because they were afraid they would be embarrassed ... just as they were afraid to raise their hands in school.

THE HOTLINE:

Ph: (805) 378-1494 FAX: (805) 378-1499 (8 A.M. to 1 P.M., Pacific Time, Monday through Friday)

About This Book

Painless Perfect Grammar really wrote itself. Realistically, it was written by you, those callers who have been asking questions concerning grammar, punctuation, vocabulary, and everything and anything concerned with the English language. You asked the questions, and many of them are here in *Painless Perfect Grammar*. This is truly the book of, by, and for the people. This is now the twenty-ninth year of the National Grammar Hotline. I receive up to five hundred calls each day and try to answer or return all of them within a reasonable time. What exquisite people you are for wanting to know so much about literacy and how to be literate.

Now that so many American know about the National Grammar Hotline after hearing Charlie Osgood speak about it, seeing me several times on "The Today Show," and, most recently, on "Oprah," I realized that the phone will probably ring twenty-four hours per day, every day for the rest of my life. But, that's fine. I was blessed with a wonderful education and superb teachers. This book's purpose is to clarify, to answer, and to make life more bearable through improved knowlege of our language.

I would love to hear more from you. My mailing address is Michael Strumpf, Moorpark College, 7075 Campus Road, Moorpark,

CA 93021. Please write or FAX or call. This immense world can be made so much more livable if we communicate our ideas more lucidly. If this can be done to the world, then what can we do for the world? And, that, wonderful friends, callers, and readers, is what *Painless Perfect Grammar* is all about. Finally, be aware that I wrote this book with all types of readers in mind: students, scholars, teachers, professionals, non-professionals, attorneys, doctors, journalists, writers, secretaries, bosses, in fact, everyone who speaks or writes.

Peace and Love,
Michael Strumpf

Usage, Memory Joggers, and Other Great Stuff

Just knowing words is not enough. Being able to use them properly is just as important, and it insures proper communication.

How many times have you said something or heard something said and been forced to say, "Oh, I didn't mean that!" or "What did you say? I'm not sure I know what you mean."

This chapter will attempt to point you in the right direction. It won't answer all your questions, but it will answer many. And I hope it will energize you to continue your quest for more words and more meanings.

Some of these questions from the grammar hotline had important repercussions. They not only elicited the answers to proper English usage—but also:

- saved a lady from paying her mortgage twice
- spared a secretary's job when she challenged her boss—an irate judge
- won a lawsuit

So the words in this chapter are not just language. They represent life itself.

Q. "When do I use "a" and when "an" before a noun?" an harried-sounding college student asked.

A. Did you read the question carefully? How does it sound? Awful! It should have read (as, of course, you know) "a harried-sounding college student." The rule that applies simply states you use "an" before any word that starts with either a vowel or a vowel sound.

EXAMPLES: *An* apple, *an* awful night. *An* hour. But *a* horoscope, since the *h* is sounded, unlike the *h* in "hour."

MEMORY JOGGER: Remember that "N" as in AN stands for NO consonant sound.

Q. When do you use "advice" with a *c* and "advise" with an *s*?

A. Advice—with a *c*—is a noun. I gave him some *advice*. Advise—with an *s*—is a verb. I *advise* you to listen well to my advice.

How do you remember which one is which in the heat of writing or speaking? Here are some.

MEMORY JOGGERS: "My advice is not to skate on the ice." You can remember that ICE, similar to ADVICE, is also a noun because you put an "a," "an," or "the" in front of a noun. Now for ADVISE. By remembering ICE/ADVICE/NOUN, you'll know that opposite is always with an S, and it's always a verb.

Q. "If you can straighten me out on AFFECT and EFFECT, I'll name you in my will!"

A. Effect by most lexicographers is normally stated as a noun: "The effect was noticed." However, it occasionally, only occasionally, can also be a verb but in very few and rare situations. Psychologists also speak of the "affective domain."

> ***MEMORY JOGGER:*** The word EFFECT is usually a noun. A noun usually takes a "the" in front of it. Link the "E" in th**E** to the E in EFFECT to remember. (You cannot say "the AFFECT" with an **A**.)

Q. "The other day, I said, 'I have four alternatives to choose from,' and my boss berated me. What was wrong?"
A. You were. Your boss knows that an alternative means a choice between *two* different things; it would be impossible to have four alternatives to chose from. This is a very, very common error. The word you should have used is alternates. You *can* have four alternates to choose from but never, never, NEVER four alternatives.

> ***MEMORY JOGGER:*** Alternative is reserved for two. Use alternate when there are a few.

Q. "What are the differences among antonyms, synonyms, homonyms, heteronyms, and acronyms?"
A. It's a meaty question and one that you should be able to use in your every-day life.
    Antonyms: words which are opposites—good/bad, healthy/sick, in/out.
    Synonyms: words which mean nearly the same thing—royal, regal, kingly.
    Homonyms: words which sound the same but are spelled differently: to, too, two; their, there, they're; hour, our.
    Heteronyms: words which are spelled the same but have different pronunciations and meanings—lead and lead, read and read.
    Acronyms: An acronym is the combining of the first letters of words to form new words. Here are some common ones:

PAKISTAN: Coined to represent the units to be included in the new state:
                 P–Punjab;
                 A–Afghan border states;

	K–Kashmir;
	S–Sind;
	TAN for Baluchistan
AWOL:	Absent WithOut Leave
NATO:	North Atlantic Treaty Organization
RADAR:	Radio Detecting And Ranging
SONAR:	Sound Navigation Ranging
UNESCO:	United Nations Educational, Scientific and Cultural Organization
LASER:	Light Amplification by Simulated Emission of Radiation

Q. "I wrote the following sentence: 'Let's talk a while,' and the teacher marked it incorrect. Is it?"
A. Yes. Your sentence should have read "Let's talk awhile." Awhile, one word, is an adverb which means "for a while."

A while—two words—is an article and a noun and means "a period of time." "Robert went home a while ago." "Let's sit down on the park bench awhile."

MEMORY JOGGER: Awhile—one word—Adverb
A while—two words—Noun

Since adverbs answer the five questions—"when, where, why, how, and how much"—an easy way to remember awhile as an adverb is to say to yourself AWHEN as one word, and AWHILE answers the question. "A while ago" means a period of time. "While" is now a noun, and a noun is usually preceded by "a," "an," or "the." "A while" is always two words when it is a specific period of time.

Q. "Please tell me when to use between and when to use among," an emphatic voice asked one morning. "I always get them wrong."
A. Don't feel too badly—a lot of other people do, too. But once you learn the rule, using the two words correctly is easy. Between is always used when talking about two people or things: "Between you and me." "Betweeen a rock and a hard place." Among is always used when you have three or more people or objects in your sentence: "Among the group." "Among the three of us."

MEMORY JOGGER: Link the *o* in group with the *o* in among. That should help you to remember that among is always used when you are discussing groups of three or more.

Q. "I received notification from my mortgage company asking for bimonthly payments. What do they mean? I don't want to pay my mortgage twice a month."

A. Bimonthly can mean "twice a month," or it can mean "every two months." You had better contact your mortgage company and ask for a clarification.

> NOTE: Whether the word means twice a month or every two months, the spelling remains the same.

MEMORY JOGGER: It's easy to remember that "bi" means two if you simply remember that a bicycle has two wheels.

Q. "Can you help me keep *capital* and *capitol* straight?"

A. A good memory tickler is to recall that a *capitol* is "a building or group of buildings in which the government meets," and it usually has a dome. Think of the *o* in capitol and the *o* in dome. All else is *capital:* capital punishment, capital sin, capital as in money, capitalism, capital as in the uppermost part of a column or pilaster, etc.

Q. "My Mother Superior told me that I have catholic tastes, and I automatically thought she meant that I liked fish on Fridays, even though we have given up that habit, but not our other habits," asked a nun from a Catholic high school. "However, she thought her comment was most jocular and amusing. Why?"

A. I would love to meet the Mother Superior because obviously she has a superior sense of humor. "Catholic," in the sense she was using, is spelled with a lower-case *c*, and means "universal, general, all-inclusive, broad, and comprehensive." The word comes from the Greek word *holos* meaning "whole." If you can remember holos, whole, you will remember that a person with catholic tastes likes the whole of everything.

Q. "I always get these two words confused—*compliment* and *complement*. Can you give me an easy way to remember them?"
A. For me, that's very easy, and it will be for you, too. I always remember *complement* by remembering *complete*. And then I just remember that *compliment*, with the *i*, is something *I* like to hear. Complement, of course, means "to finish, or complete." I hope everyone knows what compliment means. If you don't, or you haven't had one recently, look it up!

Q. "Can you *counsel* me on the word *council* and the difference between the two words?"
A. *Council* means "an assembly of persons called together for consultation or discussion." *Counsel* is "the exchange of ideas, opinions, advice, or guidance" that the council might come up with. A lawyer is often called a counsel because he or she counsels or gives advice.

MEMORY JOGGER: The City Council can be remembered by linking CI in city and the CI in council. COUNSEL can be brought to mind by linking the SEL with one who SELLS advice, such as a lawyer.

Q. "What is the singular of *datum?*"
A. *Datum* is singular. It is one item of fact. If you wish to use the plural of datum, it's *data*. Similarly, *medium* is singular—*media* is plural. *Stratum* is singular and *strata* is plural. We'll give you examples and memory joggers in a while. (Two words—a while—remember?) *Criterion* is singular. *Criteria* is plural. *Alumnus* is singular, masculine. *Alumna* is a feminine singular. *Alumni* is the plural form of the masculine singular, and *alumnae* is the plural form for the feminine singular.
    REMEMBER that with the singular form we must use single predicates (verbs). Therefore:

The datum is important.
The criterion is necessary.
The alumnus is wealthy.
The alumna is even wealthier.
The television medium is often full of tedium.
The rock stratum is very thick.

Now for the plurals.

The many criteria are vital for our decision.
Thge computer data are fascinating.
The alumnae are returning to the college.
The media necessary for mass communication are composed of
    radio, TV, newspapers, and the internet.
The rock strata are difficult to penetrate.

Q. "I always get confused with the spellings and pronunciations of *desert* and *dessert*. It's driving me crazy."
A. *Desert* has two pronunciations and two meanings. It can mean "a wasteland," in which case the stress is on the first syllable. Or it can mean "to abandon," in which case the stress is on the second syllable. *Dessert* is pronounced the same way as the second meaning of desert. The word with *two* esses has only *one* meaning, but the word with one *s* has two meanings.

Q. "Harvard is *different than* Yale is. Is that correct?"
A. No. No. It is most definitely a major error, one that is perpetrated by users of the English language in and out of school. The answer is: "Harvard is *different from* Yale."

MEMORY JOGGER: Link the "FF's" in "DIFFERENCE" to the "F" in "FROM." Different *from*.

Q. "What does *directive counseling* mean? My analyst says that he is *non-directive*."
A. I asked this caller if there were long periods of silence during the

hour she spent with her analyst, and she said "yes." I then offered a short parable to illustrate the difference between "directive" and "non-directive" counseling.

On a wharf overlooking a lake sat a directive counselor and a non-directive counselor. The directive counselor accidentally fell into the water. He went down once and came up. He went down twice and came up. As he was about to go down for the third time, he called "help," and the non-directive counselor dove in and pulled him out.

Later, as they were towelling off in the locker room, the directive counselor said: "Thank you for saving my life. I almost drowned." The non-directive counselor said, "It's a good thing you called for help."

Does this explain the difference between the two? If not, a brief explanation. A *directive* counselor constantly asks questions to which the patient offers answers. The *non-directive* counselor waits for the client to show or exhibit a need. If the directive counselor had not called "help," the non-directive counselor would have let him drown. Therefore, a non-directive counselor will wait, perhaps for hours, for the patient to say something.

Q. "What is the meaning of the word *encouch?* My boss has been dictating this word to me for years and years. And I have been blithely writing it down, and accepting it as a word, since he's so well educated; he's a lawyer, a judge, and a state senator."

A. I asked the caller how he used the word. She replied, "Here is his sentence: 'I encouch my ideas in certain phraseology.' " I looked up the word in not only my *Oxford,* but also my *Webster's,* and my *American Heritage Dictionary.* The word never appeared. Then I went into my *Blackstone* law dictionary and then to the *Ballantine Law Dictionary.* No such word existed! The poor judge had unwittingly mixed up the words *encroach* and *couch* in his mind. Encroach, of course, means "to intrude," and couch means "to arrange, to place."

This only serves to illustrate how many of us, because of the academic degrees that we have and the years of education that we've endured, stop questioning ourselves. But so much of education today is gobbledy-gook. For heaven's sake, don't think that, because you have college degrees, you know it all, or if you don't, that you're totally ignorant.

Q. "When do you use *farther?* And when do you use *further?*"
A. *Farther* is always used to denote actual distance in space. "He is farther ahead than I." "How much farther do we have to go?" *Further* denotes distance in abstract ideas. "We are further from the solution than ever." "I have nothing further to suggest."

MEMORY JOGGER: The FAR in FARTHER will always serve to remind that this word refers to distance.

Q. "What is the difference between *flammable* and *inflammable?*"
A. What an absurd language we have at times! The prefix *in* should stand for "not." Therefore, inflammable *should* mean "not flammable." But it doesn't. *Flammable* things can catch fire, and *inflammable* things can burst into flame. Be careful around either kind.

Q. "How can I *insure* that I never use *ensure* incorrectly again?"
A. *Ensure* is really just a variation of *insure*. But it has a subtle shading of meaning. Insure means, of course, to cover with insurance. When you want to "make something safe and secure, or to guarantee," you are better off using the word ensure. (But it's not incorrect to use insure.) Ensure comes from the Norman French *enseurer*, perhaps a variant of the Old French *asseurer*, meaning "to assure."

Q. "My friend said, 'the *less* friends one has, the more he can pay attention to himself.' Is 'less' correct here? It sounds funny."
A. You have a very sharp ear. I wish more people were able to discern between two similar but different words. *Fewer* is used for items that can be counted. *Less* is used for quantities that can be measured. Your friend should have said, "the fewer friends one has. . ." By the way, radio announcers make this mistake all too often.

MEMORY JOGGER: "When you barbecue, use fewer skewers for less mess."

Q. "*Lie* and *lay* always provide a source of confusion. Any pointers?"
A. These two little words—lie and lay—belie their true meanings.

   Lay means to put down: "Today, I lay the book down. Yesterday, I laid the book down. I have laid the book down." *Lie* means to make oneself horizontal: "Today, I lie down. Yesterday, I lay down. Between yesterday and today, I have lain down." What confuses many people is that the past tense of lie is the same word as the present tense of lay.

MEMORY JOGGER: Lay means to put or pLAce down. The LA in pLAce can remind you to use "lay." Lie means to rest, lie down, or recline. Rest brings relief. The IE in relIEf should remind you that rest goes with LIE. So say to yourself LAY—pLAce; LIE—relIEf.

Q. "*Loan* and *lend* often confuse people. Any answers?"
A. *Loan* is usually a noun. "He gave me a loan." The verb is *lend.* "I'll lend you the money, but I won't 'loan' it to you." In the past tense, I *lent* you money. Not *loaned!* There is no such word as loaned except, alas, in business usage. the banks have (ugh!) taken liberties and are using loaned as a verb. those bankers will say, "the banks loaned money." Go to your local bank and tell them that lend is better than loan. However, loan, as a verb in the present tense, is becoming more and more acceptable, expecially when pertaining to money.

MEMORY JOGGER: To remember LENT, connect it with CENT. "I only lent him a cent."

Q. "As a student nurse, I don't know whether I should ask '*May* I have your bedpan?' or '*Can* I have your bedpan?' "
A. The anwer is: use *may.* It implies the granting of permission. *Can* implies the ability to do something.

Q. "I am a chef, and I've seen both *morel* and *morelle.* Is there a difference?"

A. There most certainly is. And, to be dramatic, it's the difference between life and death. *Morel* is any of the various edible mushrooms. *Morelle* is an extremely poisonous growth.

Q. "I have just been to the doctor, and he told me he wants to *palpitate* my big toe. What does he mean?"
A. I think your doctor used the wrong word, or you heard him incorrectly. Next time you see him, please correct him. *Palpate* means "to touch or feel or probe." *Palpitate* means "to pound heavily." I'm sure your doctor wants to palpate your big toe, which may make your heart palpitate as you anxiously wait for him to discover something you hope is not there.

Q. "How about *principal* and *principle*. I'm always correcting my 6th grade students. Make it easy for me—and them."
A. One of the meanings of *principle* is "most important." The principal of a school is, as head of the school, the most important person in it.

MEMORY JOGGER: Link the "LE" in "ruLE" with the LE in PRIN-CIPLE, and you should always remember that PRINCIPLE means a basic truth, assumption, law, or ruLE.

We can remember princiPAL by saying, "My pal is the princiPAL of the school."

Q. "In the incredible magic show I just saw, a woman was being levitated. Was she *raising* or *rising* from the stage?"
A. She was *rising* from the stage. She could be *raised* by someone else, or something else, but no one could "rise" her. Rising is something people have to do by themselves.

MEMORY JOGGER: Link the "I" in rise to I, alone. You can do it by yourself. You can rise from the sofa. But if you're going to raise something, someone or something has to do it.

Q. "Which is correct, *regardless* or *irregardless?*"

A. For many years *regardless* was the only correct choice. It means, of course, "without regard for, not caring." *Irregardless* was considered totally wrong because it contained a double negative: it literally says not not caring. This particular word really illustrates how our language changes and is changing. Public pressure and wide usage of IRREGARDLESS have brought about acceptance. The people who speak our glorious language like IRREGARDLESS. Therefore, suffice it to say, that irregardless is now a permanent part of the English language. But you will never, never hear it from my lips! I may not like it personally, but don't feel guilty if you're used to using it.

Q. "When should I use *shall* and when *will?*"

A. The first person singular and plural (*I* and *we*) take *shall*. All the other forms use *will*. The only time *will* is used with *I* or *we* is to show a strong intent. An example: "I will escape no matter what you do to stop me."

Q. "My mother is president of the PTA. The other night, she used the sentence 'How can you be so *sophomoric* in your attitude towards boys?' I automatically said, 'Mom, I'm only a Freshman.' And my mother laughed and laughed but didn't tell me what was so funny. Can you?"

A. I chuckled, also. The sense in which mom used the word is a direct derivation from Sophocles, one of the great playwrights of ancient Greece. *Sophomoric* means "foolish." What mom was really saying was "Why aren't you wiser about your relationships with boys?"

Q. "Can I *take* something to the store or should I *bring* it to the store?"

A. This question has arisen many, many times. *Take* means "to carry away from."

> **MEMORY JOGGER:** Link the "A" in "TAKE" and the "A" in "AWAY" to remember take away. DO the same with the BR in "brought" and the BR in "bring," to remember that if something can be brought to you, the correct word is "bring." So I told this woman to TAKE her husband's lunch to his store.

Q. "When should I use *than* and when *then*?"
A. *Than* is used when we are comparing two clauses which are not equal. "Pie is richer than cake." *Then* is used to answer the question "when?"

> **MEMORY JOGGER:** Then—when? Focus on the "A" in "compAre" and the "A" in thAn.

Q. "I'm in the midst of a lawsuit. We think we know the correct answer, but we want to verify it. What does the *slash mark* (/) or *virgule* mean? There is a statement in our suit: 'The welders/assemblers will receive a raise of 14% per annum.' "
A. The slash mark, or virgule, simply means "and/or" which, translated in legal jargon, implies that both groups will receive the raise in pay. I'm sure this information could have come from a dictionary, but the fact that I was called proved the caller did not trust the lexicon, or didn't have the time/patience to consult it. Actually one of the lawyers involved argued that the slash mark meant "or," not "and/or." He wanted to give the raise to either the welders or the assemblers, not both. When I answered the question, they both got pay raises.

Q. "When is *y* a vowel?"
A. Has any teacher told you when *y* is used as a vowel? I'll bet the answer is no. And I'll bet most teachers don't know. Here's one you can use to upstage your friends! "Y" is considered a vowel WHEN THERE IS NO OTHER VOWEL IN THE SYLLABLE OR THE

WORD. You know what a SYLLABLE is, don't you? A syllable is a sound division. There are as many syllables in a word as there are separate sounds in a word when spoken. Look at this word:

ONOMATOPOETICALLY

Now, let's break it up into sounds, or, if you like, syllables. Remember, every syllable has to have at least one letter, and every syllable has to have at least one vowel. So, if it's a one letter syllable, that letter must be a vowel—or a "Y."

Now, we're going to syllabicate it—or break it up:

ON-O-MAT-O-PO-ET-IC-AL-LY

Notice in the last syllable that LY is a separate sound unit. Therefore, it needs a vowel. But all we have is a "Y." In this case, then, "Y" becomes the vowel.

Those Grammar Questions

Most of the people who called the National Grammar Hotline with the following questions didn't even have a passing acquaintance with grammar—the tools one needs to speak or write the English language correctly.

They must have been asleep or absent when their grammar school teachers explained the basics, if the basics were, indeed, ever properly explained. If you fall into this category, don't despair. I promise you an easy journey through terrain that has blocked many a well-educated graduate—and that includes public speakers, radio and TV announcers, and many authority figures who assault our ears daily with just plain bad English.

For some reason, the word grammar scares people. But it needn't. Here are the A-B-C's—the very *least* you should know. There are eight basic parts of speech. They are:

NOUN: the name of a person, place or thing. (Most people seem to *know* this one—perhaps because Noun/Name is easy to remember.)
VERB: this word expresses action or being. It jumps, stands, dances, or is.

ADJECTIVE: describes a noun or a pronoun. (If English were logical it would be called an **ADNOUN**).**

ADVERB: describes a verb, an adjective, or another adverb, usually tells how something is done, and usually ends in *ly*.

PREPOSITION: forms a phrase with the noun which is its object, but is really an adverb—*in* the morning, *to* the school, *from* the room, *by* the car.

CONJUNCTION: joins words or sentences together.

INTERJECTION: expresses excitement or emotion.

PRONOUN: is a word that takes the place of a noun. Such as "they" for "kids," or "she" for "Heather."

What you've just read is absolutely essential for what you are about to read. You must be sure that you're on solid ground before you take a step forward. Therefore, each step of the way, I'm going to ask you to go back and review to be sure that the material we have covered is implanted in your mind and that reasonable understanding is present. And, if you are still puzzled, telephone me.

Q. "A British friend sat in on one of my classes at the college and said, 'In England, we call verbs *predicates*. What do you call them here?' What are the similarities and differences between the two?"

A. A predicate is a verb that is married to a noun, that is done by the noun. In the clause, the noun is called the *subject*, and the verb is called the *predicate*. So a verb is single, unattached. A predicate is married and part of the clause. EXAMPLES: Here are some verbs: run, sit, lie, eat, love, learn. Now let's make these into predicates: I rand down the block. I sit on the steps. I eat the pie, etc. Now, "ran," "sit," and "eat" are predicates because they are married to "I"—the subject. When a verb is by itself, unattached, unmarried, it is called a verb. As soon as you put that verb into a sentence, its name changes to

---

**It's our contention that the unknown Latin grammarian who named the word ADJECTIVE actually said AD—and then sneezed—*jective*. It's obvious to everyone but spoilsports that he/she meant to say and should have said ADNOUN. Although this word already exists, it does so with a different meaning. We feel strongly that our definition, a word that describes a noun, should be added to the lexicon.

"predicate." In addition to "action" words, whenever you see these words:

IS   ARE   WAS   WERE   HAS BEEN   HAVE BEEN
HAD BEEN   WOULD HAVE BEEN   COULD HAVE BEEN
SHOULD HAVE BEEN   AM,   *AND OTHERS,*
and you know that you have a predicate (verb), and there's no more guesswork involved.

Q. "Is there an *easy* method to find *subjects* and *predicates* in sentences and to make them agree?"
A. Of course there is. Here is a sentence: "The building burned." What is the action word? The answer is "burned." "Burned" is therefore the predicate (verb). What burned? The answer is "building." That is the subject. Since *building* is singular, the correct predicate (verb) is "is." That is, of course, simple. Anyone can understand it.

The problem occurs when a prepositional phrase is located between the subject and the predicate.

EXAMPLE: The building on the docks (is) (are) burning. "On the docks" is a prepositional phrase. You might be tempted to make "docks"—which is plural—agree with the predicate (verb) and to make that plural too. But that would be wrong. Always drop the prepositional phrase out of your sentence before attempting to make subject and predicate (verb) agree. Then it becomes easy. Once you drop "on the docks" out of the sentence, you're left with "The building . . . is burning." It quickly becomes obvious that *building* is the subject, and a singular predicate (verb) is required. Here are some more difficult examples:

A HANDFUL OF TANNED, BOISTEROUS BOYS AND GIRLS (was) (were) IN THE POOL.

YOUR INTERFACE WITH MEMBERS (has) (have) AFFECTED ME.

THE BACTERIUM IN THE INTESTINAL TRACTS (is) (are) HARMLESS.

THE AREA OF MY STRENGTHS (is) (are) . . .

In the examples above, first drop out the prepositional phrases. In sentence #1, it is "of boisterous boys and girls." Now it becomes clear that "a handful . . . was."

In sentence #2, drop out "with members," and it's obvious that "Your interface . . . has."

Do the same thing with sentence #3 and #4. (The answers are: Bacterium . . . is. Area . . . is.)

Q. "How do we know the *correct* form of the predicate (v.erb) so that it agrees with the subject, as correct English dictates?"

A. All you have to remember is that if you have a singular subject, you must have a singular verb. If you have a plural subject, you must have a plural verb. Examples: "He is a great human being." *He* is singular, and *is* is singular.

"The boys are great human beings." *Boys* is plural, and the verb *are* is plural. Let's take this a little further. Here's a somewhat more complicated sentence. "He has one of those that (is) (are) rare." *One* is singular, and *that* refers back to *one*. So the verb must also be singular. The correct choice is *is*.

The common mistake most people make is to focus on the word "those"—to see it as plural—and then to choose a plural verb. But that is wrong.

Q. "What's a *preposition*, and what's a *prepositional phrase?*"

A. A preposition is a "when, where, why, how, how much" word. It's a word that also shows location or direction. Examples are: *from, to, under, over. Prepositional phrases* are groups of words starting with prepositions and ending with a noun answering the question "what," asked by the preposition. EXAMPLE: The boy fell down the stairs. The boy fell down what? "Stairs" answers the "what." Therefore *stairs* is the object of the preposition. *Down* is the preposition.

EXAMPLES of prepositional phrases:

In the morning . .
After school . . .
Down the drain . . .
To me . . .

From him . . .
Through the tunnel . . .
Between the desks . . .

If a prepositional phrase starts a sentence and the subject of the sentence is quite close to it, place a comma after the prepositional phrase.

EXAMPLE: "In the morning, I eat and wash." Notice that "I," the subject, is very close to the prepositional phrase.

Now, look at this sentence.

"In the morning came a very loud noise." Here, "noise" is the subject, and it is very far from the prepositional phrase; hence, no comma.

Q. "When I say to the jury . . . 'I refer you, ladies and gentlemen, to clause ten . . . ' I'm often not sure if it actually is a clause or a phrase. Will you please compare and contrast the two words for me?"

A. A clause is a group of words which contains a subject and predicate—"I see the cat." "The day is sunny." "The water is cold." There are two kinds of clauses, independent and dependent. The examples above are independent. A *dependent* clause would look like this:

"When I visit England . . . "
"After it rains . . . "

It sounds as if one shoe were falling. We're waiting for the other shoe. And yet, these dependent clauses have a subject and predicate. A phrase is a group of words with *either* a subject or predicate, not both.

EXAMPLES: . . . in the water
             . . . seeing the dog
             . . . through the evening

But, clauses in a contract are not the same as clauses in a sentence. I would guess that, as an attorney, you're probably referring to clauses, as you suspected, not phrases.

Q. "When does a person use *I* or *me* or *he* or *him* or *we* or *us?* How can an individual know when to use the right word at the right time in the right way? I'm tired of being criticized for saying 'between you and I.' "

A. We're dealing here with personal pronouns. Let's lay out these personal pronouns for you so that you can see what they look like, and then we'll discuss how they're used.

Personal pronouns are divided into three cases, nominative, objective, and possessive.

NOMINATIVE CASE:

    I, You, He, She, It, We, You, They, Who, Whoever

OBJECTIVE CASE:

    Me, You, Him, Her, It, Us, You (plural), Them, Whom, Whomever

POSSESSIVE CASE:

    Mine, Yours, His, Her, Its, Our, Your, Their

At this point, it is very necessary to stress that grammar and the proper use of it are similar to proper driving habits and obeying the law. In both instances, knowledge must be learned prior to the application of that knowledge. This involves work, and that's what we're asking you to do at this point.

Nominative case pronouns are used as the subjects of sentences: She ate the cake. *She* is the subject; therefore, it is in the nominative case. Nominative case pronouns are also used as predicate nominatives. For example: The boys are *they. They* is a predicate nominative—meaning the word *they* renames the word *boys,* the subject of the sentence. Another example: It is he. *He* is a predicate nominative renaming *it*—the subject. These proper constructions will probably sound awkward to ears that have been hearing the incorrect pronouns for so many years. Why not record some proper pronoun usages on a cassette and practice listening to English correctly used? Also, listen to others misuse our language and, if you do not have the temerity to correct them, at least make a mental note of their error. To explain *objective pronouns* thoroughly would involve a tremendous amount of unnecessary verbiage. Instead, I'm going to give you a number of examples, and, if you simply copy these examples in your speaking and writing, you will be using the language correctly:

1 "She saw *him.*"
2 "I went to visit *her.*"
3 "Seeing *me* made the people happy."
4 "To love *her* is a pleasurable experience."
5 "We gave *him* the book."

The objective case, as the above examples illustrate, is used as the object of the sentence. Note that in illustration #2, *to visit her, to visit* is an infinitive and begins the phrase while *her* ends it. In illustration #3, *Seeing me,* a gerund phrase, finishes with *me.* In #4, *to love her,* the last word in this infinitive phrase must be *her,* an object. In the three examples, the last word is the object of the phrase, the objective case of the pronoun.

The *possessive case* is so simple as to require little or no explanation. It is used to show possession or ownership. For example: "The couch is *hers.*" "The book is *mine.*" "This is *my* car." "These are *their* cucumbers."

Q. "When does one use *who* or *whom?*"
A. See the section on pronouns above. *Who* is in the *nominative* case and is therefore always used as the subject for a sentence. *Whom* is in the *objective* case and is always the object of a sentence.

FOR EXAMPLE: "Who is it?" "Who called?" "Who gave you the ticket?" "You gave it to whom?" "Please give it to whomever you wish."

NOTE: It is not bad form to use *who* exclusively, ignoring *whom.* In fact, the use of *whom* is dying out. It just depends upon what tone you want to convey. In formal use, *whom* is still very much desired.

Q. "When do you use *done* and when do you use *finished* when referring to the end of a task?"
A. I'm glad you brought that up. I'm sick of hearing people say, "We're done with our food," or "I'm done with the newspaper." How awkward this sounds! Of course, they should have said "finished." Why? The word *finished* means to end a job, to complete something. For example: "We finished our dinner." "He finished reading the newspaper." Done is the past participle form of the verb "to do," and can only be used adjectivally to describe a noun. Look at these sentences and the explanations which follow each.

The job is done. This is correct, as *job* is being described by *done*, a past participle used here as a predicate adjective separated from the subject by the intransitive verb-predicate *is*.

I am done. Wrong because here, *done* is not describing *I*. It cannot be used as a predicate adjective. *I am finished*, or *I have done it*, or *I did it*, are preferable. In these sentences, *finished*, *done*, or *did* are verbs, not adjectives.

Q. "What is a *conjunction*, and are there different types?"
A. A *conjunction* is a joining word. If it joins word to word or clause to clause, it is a *coordinating* conjunction.

EXAMPLES: and, but, or, nor, for, yet, so.
The man *and* his dog sat by the fire.

And is a coordinating conjunction because it joins man and dog.

Another example: "The man read, and the dog slept." *The man read* is an independent clause; *the dog slept* is an independent clause. The word *and* joins one to the other, and is a coordinating conjunction here, also. Here is an example of a *subordinating* conjunction:

"*After* the man read, he was exhilarated."

Some additional examples: "Although the student had a difficult time in school, he still managed to learn grammar because it was important to him." *Although* is a subordinating conjunction, because it begins a dependent clause ending with the word *school*. *Because* is a subordinating conjunction also, starting a dependent clause ending with the word *him*.

Q. "Is *defense* a verb? I hear it on television all the time."

A. Can you defense something, as in football? Or can you defense yourself? The answer is NO. Defense is a noun, even though it is accepted as a verb in football. The preferable choice is *defend*.

Q. "How do you use *myself, himself, themselves, yourself,* etc., correctly?"

A. We use these words to reflect a noun or pronoun used earlier in the sentence, as in "He did it to himself"; or to intensify, to make stronger, the use of a noun or pronoun in a sentence. 'He himself plugged the dike." A mistake that is commonly made is: "Between him and myself...." Here, *myself* is not referring back to anything, and it is not intensifying anything. The self form cannot be used unless it *reflects back to a noun or pronoun*. The example should read: "Between him and me."

Q. "I know there are present, past, and future tenses. Do we have any other tenses in English?"

A. Of course, we have more than three tenses in English! Do we need to know them all? Well, perhaps it is necessary only for the writer or the attorney, but certainly you should be familiar with more than past, present, and future.

In my teaching experience, I have found it extremely useful to present the verb tenses on a time line, of the kind used in history classes, where an instructor places the first date over on the left and last date over on the right, with all the other dates in between. Here, then, is a "verb tense line," if you will, with the major tenses and their meaning placed in proper sequential order. This material, obviously, will involve some concentration and practice. But you certainly don't have to memorize it all at once. You can space it out over a period of time. Language is here to be used; it shouldn't be painful.

Here are some general rules and guidelines about verb tenses. All the tenses in the *indicative* mood start and stop immediately, except the *progressives*, which can continue indefinitely. All the *perfect* tenses end with the past participle form of the verb. There is an emphatic tense—simply add the word *must* to any of the tenses on the line where it makes sense. When writing, be sure to say what

INDICATIVE MOOD
ACTIVE VOICE

Beginning	Past Perfect	Past Perfect Progressive	Past	Past Progressive	Conditional Present Perfect	Present Perfect	Conditional Pres. Perf. Prog.	Present Perfect Progressive	Cond. Present	Present
Of Time	I had loved	I had been loving	I loved	I was loving		I have loved		I have been loving		I love
					I would have loved		I would have been loving		I would love	

INDICATIVE MOOD
ACTIVE VOICE

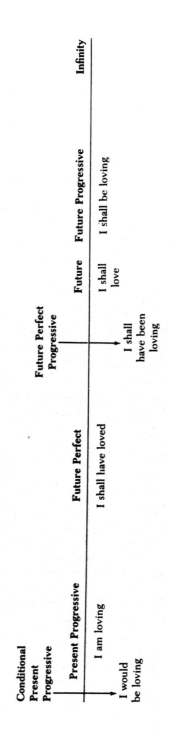

Conditional Present Progressive

Present Progressive

I am loving

I would be loving

Future Perfect

I shall have loved

Future Perfect Progressive

I shall have been loving

Future

I shall love

Future Progressive

I shall be loving

Infinity

you mean in the proper tense; if you are writing in the past tense about yesterday, then an action that occurred just before yesterday is in the past perfect (look at the time line and you'll see that past perfect is before the past, just to its left).

Q. "My son wrote this sentence at school and got a 'D.' Why? 'Lions could be heard roaring as we came close to the zoo.' "
A. This sentence is poor because the subject shifts from "lions" to "we", and the predicate shifts from passive to active. Let's improve it. "We heard lions roaring as we approached the zoo."

Here's another one from the same mother:
"When you have lots of money, one should assume s/he is lucky." This is really poor sentence structure because we have a shift in person from second to third. It would be better this way: "When one has lots of money, one should assume s/he is lucky."

One more: "The conductor once said of the orchestra that they were the best in the world."

This could be improved to: "The conductor once said of the orchestra that it was the best in the world." *Orchestra* is singular. We cannot refer to an orchestra as "they." "They" is plural.

Q. "My sergeant says I get the facts right, but I put them down poorly," a local policeman told me. " 'She ran after the cat wearing curlers' That *is* what happened. What does the sergeant mean?"
A. This is what we call a misplaced modifier. The "wearing curlers" is in the wrong place. It should read: "Wearing curlers, she ran after the cat."

Here's another illogical sentence:
"The exterminator attracts ants with the smell of honey." This means that the ants smell of honey. That's not what we meant to say. Let's correct it: "The exterminator, with a smell of honey, attracts ants." No, that still won't do. The *exterminator* has the smell of honey. It should be: "The exterminator uses the smell of honey to attract ants."

Here's one we particularly like:
"She borrowed a tomato from a friend that was rotten."
This should be changed to either "She borrowed a rotten tomato

from a friend," or "She borrowed a tomato from a rotten friend," depending on the facts of the case.

Q. "What is a *split infinitive?* I learned it years past in school, and I want to explain it to my son."
A. An infinitive is the word "to" plus the verb form: to run, to sit, to walk, to eat. A *split infinitive* occurs when one places an adverb between the word "to" and the verb. So a split infinitive would look like this: "to easily run the mile," "to quickly drink the wine." Let's revise these so they're no longer split. "To run the mile easily," "to drink the wine quickly."

The infinitive can—but should not—be split in other ways. "One should try to, if one can, eat a piece of melon every day." That's a ridiculous sentence. Let's revise it. "If one can, one should try to eat a piece of melon every day." These are the two major ways in which infinitives can be split. Don't use either.

Q. "What's a *dangling participle?* My daughter's teacher explained to her, but she still doesn't understand."
A. Remember what a participle is? A participle is a word that used to be a verb and is now used as an adjective. There are two kinds of participles, present and past. Present participles always end in "ing"— writing, swimming, jumping, eating. To form the past participle of any verb, put "have," "has," or "had" in front of the present tense of the verb. For example, place "have" in front of "lose." What happens to "lose?" It becomes "lost." Cross off the word "have." Lost is the past participle. Let's try a few more. "Have see." "See" becomes "seen." Cross off the "have." *Seen* is the past participle. "Have look." "Look" becomes "looked." *Looked* is the past participle.

Let's get into dangling.

"Driving my car, a mountain lion ran after me."

"Driving" is a present participle, but it is misplaced, or *dangling*.

The mountain lion wasn't driving my car. I was. So let's rewrite the sentence properly. It can be done in many different ways. For instance: "I, driving my car, was chased by a mountain lion." Awkward. Let's do better. "While driving my car, I was chased by a mountain lion." That's better, and nothing is dangling.

Let's try another one. "Drinking at an outdoor restaurant, Tel Aviv exhibits itself beautifully."

Now, obviously, Tel Aviv is not drinking at an outdoor restaurant. The present participle is "drinking," but it belongs in a different part of the sentence. So it should be written: "Tel Aviv exhibits itself beautifully to a tourist drinking at an outdoor restaurant."

I'm sure you've all heard of *participial phrases*. A participial phrase is a group of words starting with a participle and ending with a noun called the *object of the participle*. The participle is always the *first* word of every participial phrase, and the object of the participle, a noun or pronoun, is always the *last* word of the participial phrase.

Two examples: The boy driving my car is my son.

Driving is the participle. *Car* is the object of the participle. *Driving my car* is the participial phrase.

"I saw a man eating his hat." *Eating* is the participle. *Hat* is the object of the participle. *Eating his hat* is the participial phrase.

Why is it important to know about participial phrases? The answer we are about to give applies to a lot of information in this chapter.

Writing, like painting or playing the piano, is an art form. Before one can apply paint to canvas, s/he must first learn how to mix paint so the proper shades can be achieved. Musicians constantly practice scales before they attempt to play concertos. The scale, the mixing of paints on a palette, are the rudiments of an art form. They're the basics. In writing, the basics involve learning the structure of the language, so that one can write within that structure without paying attention, so that grammar is no longer an impediment to creativity.

Q. "I was taught that in the sentence 'He is running' the word 'he' is the *subject* and 'is' is the *predicate*. Right? In that case, what is the word 'running'? I was also taught that verbs are action words. Running is an action word. Is it also a verb, along with the word 'is'?"
A. I suggest that you refer to the question in this book dealing with verbs, and that will show you quite clearly what the different verbs look like so they can be readily identified. However, "running" is *not* considered a verb. It is one of the several types of "verbals." A verbal is a word which *used to be* a verb. It is now a different part of speech. There are three kinds of verbals: gerunds, infinitives, and participles.

A *gerund* always ends in -ing and is used as a noun: running, sitting, walking, eating.

> EXAMPLE: *Running* is fun. *Running* is the subject of the sentence. It is used as a noun. Therefore, it is a gerund.

Infinitives consist of the word "to" plus a verb: to run, to sit, to eat.

> EXAMPLE: to run is fun. "To run" is the subject of the sentence. "Is" is the predicate.

Participles are of two types, present and past. The former always ends in "-ing"; the latter can have many different endings. All participles are used as adjectives.

> EXAMPLE: *"The beaten man survived his attack."* *Beaten* is a past participle. It is describing *man*, which is a noun, and therefore "beaten" is used as an adjective.

Q. "What is the difference between a *direct object* and an *indirect object*? My English teacher mentioned it in class, and I didn't know what she was talking about."
A. A direct object is a noun or pronoun that receives the action of the verb.

> EXAMPLE: She opened the book. *Book* is a direct object because it receives the action (of opening).

> SECOND EXAMPLE: He cleaned the table. *Table* is a direct object because it received the cleaning.

An indirect object is a noun or pronoun which receives the direct object and normally precedes the direct object in the sentence.

> EXAMPLE: She gave Bob the money. *Bob* is the indirect object because he received the money—the direct object. We threw *them* the football. *Them* is an indirect object because "they" received the football, which is the direct object.

Q. "What *other types of objects* are there?"
A. There are *objects of prepositions:*

". . . under the *table*"
". . . from the *school*"
". . . between the *children*."

In the above phrases *from, under* and *between* are the prepositions. *Table, school,* and *children* are the objects of the prepositions.
There are objects of gerunds or present participles:

". . . running the *mile*"
". . . eating the *dinner*."

In these examples *running* and *eating* are gerunds or present participles. *Mile* and *dinner* are the objects of the gerunds or participles. And, finally, there are objects of infinitives:

". . . to run the *mile*."
". . . to eat the *dinner*."

In this instance, *to run* and *to eat* are infinitives. *Mile* and *dinner* are the objects of the infinitives.

Q. "In the dictionary, I have seen "VT" and "VI" after verbs. What do these abbreviations mean?"
A. *VT* stands for "verb, transitive." *VI* stands for "verb, intransitive." *Transitive* means that a verb can take a direct object. "I hit the desk." *Hit* is a transitive verb because it is doing something to the desk, which is a direct object. *Intransitive* verbs are known by several other names, such as *linking* or *joining* verbs. Intransitive verbs link or join subjects to predicate nouns or predicate adjectives.

EXAMPLE: "The storm was a violent one."

Storm is the subject, *was* is the intransitive verb; *one* is the predicate nominative.

Q. "How can I learn to write shorter letters? The letters I receive are so long that it takes too much time to read them, and I sympathize with other executives who have to read mine."

A. I took a sentence from a letter which read as follows:

"I am the president of a large corporation.
The name of the corporation is the XYZ Corporation."

I modified the sentence to read:

"I am the president of XYZ, a large corporation."

I tightened up the rest of his letter similarly by the use of *appositives*. An appositive is a word or phrase that re-identifies a noun or phrase and follows it directly, or almost directly, in a sentence. For instance: in the sentence above, "XYZ" is an appositive. Some additional examples:

She lives in a new apartment complex, Parklabrea.
She went to a fascinating city, San Francisco.
He bought a Cadillac, a prestigious car.

"Parklabrea," "San Francisco" and "a prestigious car" are all appositives.

Q. "My hero, the quarterback of the university's football team, said, 'We were badder than them.' Is this correct?"

A. It's not correct, although "bad" is now common slang for "good." There is no such word as *badder*. He should have said "worse"—if that's what he meant. Other examples of this usage are: good, better, best; bad, worse, worst; nice, nicer, nicest. If an athlete, or any role model for that matter, opens his or her mouth, we expect that the person who speaks is educated well enough to speak correctly.

Q. "Please compare and contrast *predicate adjectives* and *predicate nominatives* for me. Do they have anything to do with predicates?"

A. I hope so, because they have the word "predicate" in their name, but only *indirectly* are they related to the predicate. A "predicate nominative" is a noun that re-names the subject and is separated from the subject by the predicate: *John is a genius*. *Genius* re-names *John*. John is the subject—*genius* is the predicate nominative.

A "predicate adjective" is an adjective that describes the subject, and is separated from the subject by the predicate. *That building is beautiful and old*. *Beautiful* and *old* are both predicate adjectives because they both describe the subject *(building)* and are separated from it by the predicate *(is)*.

Q. "My boss dictated this sentence, and I think something is wrong with it: 'The writers in our population are sure that they can influence the people who read them.' I'm not sure what word 'they' refers back to."

A. You are questioning the meaning of the word *antecedent*. The antecedent is the noun in a sentence to which the pronoun in the same sentence refers. In the above sentence, *they* has two possible antecedents—*writers* and *population*—which could give this sentence two totally different meanings. Who is going to influence the people? The population or the writers? And what is the antecedent of them— the writers or the population?

Please observe this rule in your own writing and perhaps try to suggest it to your boss: *keep nouns as close as possible to their antecedents*. In this way, unnecessary words causing confusion will not get between the pronoun and the antecedent.

Q. "How do you diagram a sentence?"

A. I thought diagramming was dead until several years ago, when I began to receive a flood of telephone calls on the subject. From the calls, it would appear that more and more people would like to return to this method of understanding English. If it helps, fine; if it doesn't help, then just skip over this section.

The basic diagram for a sentence is a vertical line bisected by a horizontal line, with the subject on the left and the predicate on the right. Here is an example:

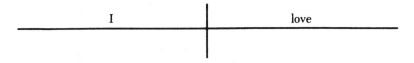

If you have a compound subject or a compound predicate, it would be diagrammed as follows:

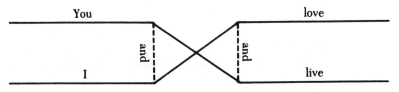

Any adjectives are simply put below the nouns that they modify, and any adverbs are placed beneath the verbs, adjectives, or other adverbs that they modify, as you can see in the example:

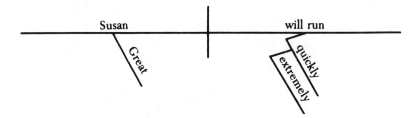

A sentence with a direct object would be diagrammed as follows:

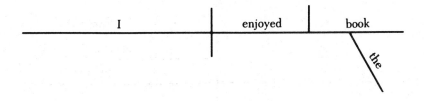

Similarly, here's how you would diagram a predicate nominative and following that, a predicate adjective.

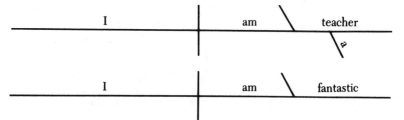

Nouns of direct address are diagrammed like this.

Appositives, like this:

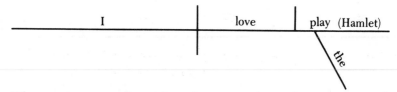

When we join two independent clauses together to form a compound sentence, we would have a diagram like this:

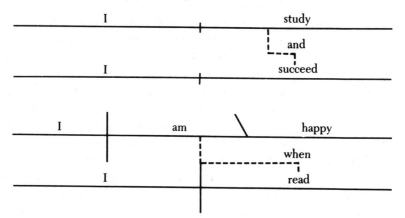

Some of us are picture-oriented. Many of us can understand something if we can see it in an illustration or photograph, or in this case a diagram. What I used to do, once I became proficient at the basic technique of diagramming sentences, was to mentally picture a sentence laid out, with each word neatly placed in its own spot, with a special line indicating whether it was an appositive, or direct object, or whatever. One aspect of this, I might add, is that one tends to speak a little less and a little more carefully and a little more slowly.

Most Commonly Misused Words

Vocabulary can be entertaining. David Larsen illustrated the point in his *Los Angeles Times* column "Around the Southland" when he observed that if a lawyer is disbarred, and a priest is defrocked, what about an electrician? Is he de-lighted, a musician de-noted, a cowboy de-ranged, a model de-posed and a medium dispirited? Why don't you fill in the rest. (Our answers are on the bottom of this page, upside down.)

1. A Far East diplomat is	8. A podiatrist
2. An office worker	9. A songwriter
3. A banker	10. A printer
4. Politicians	11. A detective
5. Wine merchants	12. A maestro
6. A baker is	13. A florist
7. A school teacher	

1. disoriented	7. degraded
2. defiled	6. unrolled
3. disinterested	5. deported
4. devoted	4. devoted
5. deported	3. disinterested
6. unrolled	2. defiled
7. degraded	1. disoriented
8. defeated	
9. decomposed	
10. depressed	
11. dissolved	
12. disconcerted	
13. deflowered	

Q. " 'I sit *besides* Jim at school,' my son said the other day, and I tried to correct him, but failed."

A. *Beside* and *besides* mean two different things. Your son should have used *beside*, which means "at the side of", and reserved *besides* for "in addition to." "I sat beside Jim at school. No one sat besides us because we had the only chairs."

Q. "My boss said I have the *capacity* to be a good architect if I would hone my drafting *ability*. It seemed to me as though he was contradicting himself."

A. No, he wasn't. *Capacity* in the sense that he used it means "potential, the future power to do something," as contrasted with abilities, which are the skills you have now.

Q. "When I *censor* a letter, in my duties as an Army captain, am I also *censuring* it?"

A. You might be, since *censuring* means "blaming, finding fault with, or criticizing." But that wouldn't really be the point of *censoring* the letters, which is examining them and cutting out what you consider harmful to transmit. But both a person who censures and a person who censors is called a censor (both words have the same derivation: Latin *censere*).

Q. "I review plays for my school newspaper. I wrote, 'there is a *climatic* scene in Act I' and got an 'F.' Why?"

A. I don't think your error was worth an "F." All you did was leave out a *c*. *Climatic*, the word you used, pertains to the weather (climate). Add a *c*, and you have *climactic* which pertains to a climax.

Q. "I said my brother-in-law was very *complaisant*—pleased with himself and his job and not apt to make changes easily. Was the word used correctly?"

A. You were close but not accurate. Your brother-in-law is *complacent*, or self-satisfied. The word you used, *complaisant*, means "amiable, trying to please others by his kindness, friendliness or courtesy."

Q. "Do *condom* and *condominium* both come from the same root?"
A. Definitely not! These words typify the confusion which can arise with a superficial knowledge of prefixes, suffixes and roots. Condominium is formed by combining *Con*, meaning "with", and *dominium*, meaning living—both from the Latin. It means "joint sovereignty" or "joint rule" of a territory by two or more states, and also ownership of an apartment in a larger complex. Now *condom* or *cundem* has no relationship to the Latin. This method of birth control is said to have been invented by Dr. Condom or Conton, an eighteenth century English physician. So don't automatically assume that simply because words have a similar sound, they have a similar meaning. Always check and double-check. (Or call me!)

Q. "Please straighten me out on *contemptible* and *contemptuous*. I am working with a (ditto) boss."
A. I'm sorry to hear your boss is *contemptible* ("deserving scorn or disdain") and that you are *contemptuous* ("showing or feeling scorn or disdain") of him.

Q. "I am continuously using *continual* and *continuous* incorrectly."
A. Concentrate. They're close cousins, but they have differences: *continual* means "a constant but interrupted succession," while *continuous* is "a constant and un-interrupted succession." *The continual thunderstorms* (they stopped from time to time) *and the continuous heat wave* (it didn't stop) *were depressing.*

Q. "I once sent a note to my fellow professors wishing to share some vital information with them. I started my note with these words, 'I wish to *decimate* among you . . .' Not one of them ever bothered to correct my gruesome mistake."
A. *Decimate* should have been *disseminate*. Decimate is based on the root *deca*, meaning "ten," and it means "to destroy a tenth of something." *Disseminate* means "to spread or share."

Q. "I absolutely *descry* what is going on in America today!"
A. You do? I think the word you wish to use is *decry*. Decry means "to belittle or disparage openly; to censure, to blame, and disapprove"

while *descry* means "to discern something difficult to catch sight of." "Through the fog, they could barely descry the lights of the city ahead."

Q. "Can *deprecate* and *depreciate* be used interchangeably? Seems to me they mean exactly the same thing."
A. Not at all. *Deprecate* means "to disapprove," and *depreciate* means "to lessen in price or value."

Q. "I've often seen the word *discreet* spelled *discrete* when I'm reading. Is this just an alternative spelling for the same word?"
A. No. *Discreet* and *discrete* are prime examples of our confusing language. As you know, *discreet* means "modest, lacking pretension, unobtrusive." *Discrete* means "a separate thing, individual, distinct." Two different words with different meanings, even though they are very close in spelling.

Q. "My newspaper said that a judge pronounced a verdict that was *draconian*. What does it mean? Does it have any relationship to *draconin*?
A. No, the two are completely different. A *draconian* sentence means a "harsh" or "cruel" sentence. It comes from Draco, law-giver of ancient Athens, who was said to have written his laws in blood, they were so severe. (Another form of draconian is draconic, the two meaning the same thing.) Now *draconin*, derived from mythology, is the essential element of the blood of dragons. It is a red resin.

Q. "My friend is living *elicitly* with his common-law wife. How can I convince him to get married?"
A. You can't. It's his decision. But there's nothing *elicit* about the situation—he's living *illicitly*. The first word means "to draw out" and second word means "unlawful." You might elicit his reasons for his decision to live in an illicit relationship by asking him. (Gently!) Maybe he has reasons you don't know about, which make sense to him. Ask him to be explicit!

Q. "The guy I work with in my factory says he's an *emigrant*. I say he's an *immigrant*. We have a six-pack of beer riding on the answer."
A. To be an *immigrant*, one must first be an *emigrant*. An *emigrant* is one who left one country to settle in another (from the Latin prefix *ex*, "away from", and verb "migrate", to move). When he leaves his original country he is emigrating. Once he arrives in his new country, he's known as an immigrant, from the Latin prefix *im*, meaning "in." So go and collect your six-pack because you are right. But why not split it with him? He's right, in a way. He had to emigrate to be an immigrant.

Q. What is the difference among *epitaph*, *epaulette*, and *epithet?*
A. These three words really do sound very similar, don't they? Yet they're spelled differently and have totally different meanings. But it's easy to mix them up and use them incorrectly.

An *epitaph* is what is written on your headstone. An *epithet* is a word or phrase describing someone—sometimes nicely as in "Richard the Lion-hearted," and sometimes not, as in "What's that dingbat up to now?"

An *epaulette* is the fringed piece of cloth on shoulders of a dress uniform worn by officers in the armed forces. Now you obviously would not go around asking a clergyman to write an epaulette for your headstone, would you? Nor would you spew epitaphs at people if they got you angry. Using wrong words that sound like the right ones is malapropism. For Mrs. Malaprop was a character who misused words in Sheridan's play *A School for Scandal*. And words which are misused this way are known as malapropisms, in her honor.

Q. "Didn't we used to have a *War Department* in the United States? What's it called today?"
A. We used to have a war department. But since wars can be your country's fault or the fault of the other guys' country, and no one likes to feel guilty, it was re-named. It's now called the *Department of Defense*. In any confrontation, you see, we are now simply defending ourselves. There is a term to cover this retitling of agencies of government or job titles. The word is *euphemism*. It is a nice word.

It comes from the Greek *eu,* meaning "good, or nice," and *pheme,* meaning "speech." So it literally means "nice speech." A euphemism is what we call a word which is used to replace one which doesn't sound so pleasant. Instead of calling a person an undertaker, we call him a funeral counselor. A janitor becomes a custodian. Toilet paper becomes bathroom tissue, a garbage man a sanitation worker, and so on. These are all euphemisms.

Q. "When I buy a new possession, my wife *flouts* it in front of her friends."
A. Only if she doesn't like it. *Flout* means "to treat contemptuously." What she probably does is *flaunt,* which means "to display ostentatiously."

Q. "Here's a sentence which I read in many variations from time to time which I find confusing. Help! 'The oranges were green and small, the apples large and delicious. I didn't buy the *former,* but I purchased the *latter.*' This is a simple sentence. Sometimes the sentences which I find confusing list ten or more items."
A. *Former* refers to the first of the items listed; *latter* to the second. It's easy to unravel if you link the "f" in "first" with the "f" in "former" and the "l" in latter to the "l" in "last."

Q. "I hesitate to correct the chairman of the board of our company, but he keeps referring to the 'fortuitous road which lies ahead.' Any suggestions?"
A. *Fortuitous* originally meant "accidental," although today it is generally accepted to mean "fortunate" or "lucky." Words often develop new meanings through the years as other similar or related words influence them. Here, the fortuitous-fortune link is obvious.

Some books on word usage do condemn the use of fortuitous to mean 'lucky,' but such widely read publications as *The New York Times, Times Literary Supplement,* and *Harper's Magazine* use it in the modern sense. It would be fair to say that the word has developed two definitions: the first, hardly used, and the second, its replacement.

To you, caller, I would say, "Stay quiet!" Your chairman is not incorrect.

Q. "Which is correct, 'The audience was full of praise for the singer,' or 'the audience was fulsome in its praise'?"
A. Depends on the quality of the performance. *Fulsome* means "offensively excessive or insincere." Fulsome is not equal to "full and abundant!"

Q. "My mother says my aging-hippie sister is suffering illusions. Do you think she means my sister is actually seeing things?"
A. No. Your mother's tongue slipped. She meant to say *delusions,* which denotes "false beliefs," and I would guess she is hitting out at your sister's relaxed beliefs and lifestyle. The word mom used, *illusion,* is a "false perception—a false way of seeing things."

Q. "Don't *impassable* and *impassible,* which have only one different letter, the *a* and the *i,* mean the same thing?"
A. No. *Impassable* denotes "not passable." There are no roads connecting the very tip of the island of Kauaui, so that area is impassable. On the other hand, *impassible,* with an *i,* means "incapable of suffering pain or harm; incapable of feeling."

Q. "Do I *imply* or do I *infer* that I don't care to spend the weekend away from home?"
A. *Imply* means "to suggest or hint." People will *infer* from your statement that you don't want to go. Infer means "to conclude or gather." But why imply? Why not state your feelings boldly?

Q. "I work in a bank, and the other day, I wrote a report in which I stated I thought our new checking plan was *ingenuous*. Was I correct?"
A. It's easy to mix up *ingenious* and *ingenuous,* so don't be too hard on yourself. But *ingenuous,* the word you used, means "naive, artless, open, frank," and *ingenious,* the word you wanted to use to describe the plan, means "clever, inventive, resourceful." When using words you're not too sure of, why not check them first in a good dictionary?

Q. "Do *iterate* and *reiterate* mean the same thing, 'to repeat'?"

A. Yes and no. *Reiterate* is a good example of popular usage changing the meaning of a word. Of those who use reiterate, I would guess 95 percent use it incorrectly. It does not mean "to say something again." It means "to say what's already been said again, again." *Iterate* means "to repeat" and comes from the Latin *iterare*, "to repeat." But popular usage is fast bringing about the day when iterate will be dropped entirely, and only reiterate used. But since that day hasn't come yet, it behooves (Middle English *behoven*, Old English *behofan*, "to require, be needful or fitting for") you to know the difference.

Q. " 'At this *junction* of my life, I feel disappointed at my career progress.' I wrote this for my personnel director. He suggested a night class in English. Why?"

A. Your personnel director knew that the word you should have used is *juncture*. This word means "at this point in time (usually a crisis)." *Junction*, the word you used, means "the place where two things join or meet," most usually the place where two roads or railway routes join or cross paths. Your imprecise use of the English language *may* be holding you back. Why not take the personnel director's advice?

Q. "How do you pronounce *lackadaisical?* Is it lack-adaisical or lax-adaisical?"

A. The correct answer is *lack*. Its origin is from *lackadaisy*, an expression of languor, and an extension of the term "lackaday" used to express regret. "Lackaday" came, in turn, from "Alack the day!" Someone who felt dismal about getting up in the morning was, obviously, lackadaisical. Those who pronounce the word "lax" are lax in their linguistic responsibilities.

Q. "One of my friends is always the *latest* with the gossip."

A. Your friend is always the *last* with the latest gossip. *Last* means "the final item or person in a series"; *latest* means "the most recent."

Q. "How do you pronounce *mischievous?*"

A. Mis-che-vus is the only correct pronunciation. Never say "mis-chee-vee-us." Just look at the word the next time you see it. Sometimes English words have letters that aren't pronounced, but they never have sounds that aren't shown somehow in the spelling.

Q. "What is a *mnemonic*? I think it has something to do with memory. And that's one thing I have to improve because I am a medical student."

A. A *mnemonic* is "a memory-training device." Let me give you an example. Read these words and try to remember them: kingdom, phyllum, class, order, family, genus, species, variety. Was it easy? Now read this and try to remember it: "Kings play cards on fairly good, soft velvet." Kings = kingdom; play = phyllum; cards = class; on = order; fairly = family; good = genus; soft = species; and velvet = variety. Understand: The first letter of each word in the nonsense verse was the same as each letter to be memorized in the list. And beware of *pneumonic*, an entirely different word, meaning "pertaining to the lungs or pneumonia" but pronounced very similarly.

Q. "I heard my boss say that if my typing mistakes should *reoccur*, my job would be in jeopardy. I may not be such a good typist, but I'm sure he used the word incorrectly, although I was smart enough to keep my mouth shut."

A. Your boss certainly was wrong. He meant to say *recur*. There is no such word as *reoccur*. Recur comes from the Latin *recurrere*, meaning "to run back."

Q. "What is the difference among *optician, optometrist, oculist, ophthalmologist,* and *optimist*?"

A. It is confusing, isn't it? However, an *oculist* and an *ophthalmologist* are the same: they treat diseases of the eye and require a medical degree. An *optician* makes lenses and eyeglasses; he does not prescribe or treat the eye. An *optometrist* examines, measures, and treats visual defects by means of corrective lenses or exercises that do not require a physician's license. So you are not going to a medical doctor when you're going to an optician or an optometrist. And an *optimist* is one who believes she/he can remember all of these on the first reading.

Q. "Can you *orientate* me as to the meaning of *orient?*"

A. Certainly. I can orient you—or orientate you—either one. Both are correct. Spelled with a capital *o Orient* refers to the countries of Asia. Spelled with a lower case *o* it means "to get your bearings." Orient—to get your bearings—is preferred to orientate. The opposite of the Orient—the countries of Asia—is the *Occident,* meaning the countries of Europe and the Western hemisphere.

Q. "What are the different ways in which *ough* can be pronounced, and can you give me examples?"

A. Here are some of the different pronunciations:

tough - tuff	drought - drought
thorough - thoro	cough - coff
thought - thawt	bough - bow
trough - trawff	ought - awt
slough - sluff	bought - bot
hiccough - hiccup	sought - sawt

After the phone call, which came from a high school teacher, I mused about the reason for this query. And I concluded that many of her students were simply frustrated because of the myriad of pronunciations and wanted a final answer.

George Bernard Shaw left his considerable fortune to anyone who would develop a phonetic alphabet. We have 26 letters in English, and about 44 sounds, but many ways to form the sounds using the 26 letters. *Ough* is a prime example of the confusion that can ensue when confronted with a word spelled one way and pronounced another. Would it not be easier for us to have 44 letters for the 44 sounds? GBS thought so.

Q. "Believe it or not, we have a case in the legal firm where I work involving a *pachyderm*. My somewhat precise and meticulous boss asked me this morning, 'What is a pachyderm, Sandra?' I answered, 'an elephant.' He smiled smugly and said, 'You're right, but you're wrong.' "

A. What he meant was that *pachyderm* does not mean "elephant," it means "any thick-skinned creature." An elephant *is* a pachyderm, but so are rhinoceroses and hippopotami.

Q. "People in my office keep jabbering on about the '*parameters* of this and that . . .' 'the *parameters* of the sales curve . . .', etc. I don't think they know what they're talking about, and that they often should be using the word *perimeter*. I'd like to straighten them out."

A. I'm sure you're correct in feeling they're often using this word incorrectly. As for correcting them, that's your decision; it may make you unpopular. But perhaps the satisfaction of being right is worth that risk. Let's take *perimeter* first. It is a mathematical term which denotes "the outer boundary of a body or figure." Take a piece of paper and draw a circle. The line which indicates the circle is the perimeter. *Parameter* is also a math term. It denotes "an arbitrary system, a quantity that describes a statistical population, or a characteristic element or constant factor." I would guess it is in this last sense that your office friends are using parameter. If they are describing the constant parameters of a sales curve, they are probably using parameter correctly, if sales do not vary, either up or down, but represent constant characteristics. If they are using it to describe the scope or boundaries of the sales department, the word they wish to use is perimeter. I hope this helps.

Q. "I know there's a subtle shade of difference between *persuade* and *convince*. I'm writing a report in which I have to do both. Can you explain the tinges of the meanings?"

A. In the Thorndike-Barnhart High School Dictionary, both *persuade* and *convince* mean "to get someone to do or believe something." *Persuade* emphasizes winning a person over to a desired belief or action by urging, arguing, advising, and appealing to his feelings as well as to his mind—"I knew I should study, but he persuaded me to go to the movies." *Convince* emphasizes overcoming a person's objections or disbelief by proof or arguments appealing to reason and understanding: "I convinced her to take a vacation, but I can't persuade her to do so." Persuade contains the implication of leading someone to take action, while convince restricts itself to changing a mental attitude.

Q. "The other day our club president said, '*Subsequent* to this meeting, I met with the vice-president, and we decided . . .' Surely he meant *prior*? I hear *subsequent* misused a great deal. Will you comment?"

A. *Subsequent* is currently being abused and misused; there's no doubt about it. I'm sure your president did mean "prior to . . ." or "preceding in time or order." The Latin roots are: *sub*, "close to, after," and *sequi*, "to follow," meaning together "soon after"; and *prior*, "earlier".

Q. "I am attempting my first mystery in creative writing class. I wrote, 'The body lay prone on the deck, a knife-handle clearly visible protruding from the chest.' My teacher circled 'prone' and drew two exclamation points in the margin; then she went on vacation. What's wrong?"

A. Your teacher was trying to call your attention to the meaning of the word *prone*. If the body was prone on the deck, it would be difficult to see the knife-handle protruding from the victim's chest, since prone means "lying face down." The word you should have used is *supine*. Supine means "lying face up."

MEMORY JOGGER: Use the *up* in *supine* to remind you that it means face up; prone means face down.

Q. "I think the idea of a grammar hotline is very *practicable*. I know I like getting an instant answer on the telephone, rather than trying to find it on my own."

A. I'm glad you called. If you don't mind my saying so, you find the idea of a grammar hotline *practical*, not *practicable*. These two words are easy to confuse. Practical means "sensible," and applies to both persons and things. "He is a practical man." Practicable applies to *things* only, and denotes "capable of being done."

Q. "What are the differences among *psychiatrists*, *psychologists*, and *psychoanalysts?*"
A. A *psychiatrist* is a medical doctor who studies, diagnoses, treats, and tries to prevent mental illness. He can also prescribe drugs. A *psychologist* does not have a medical degree, but attempts to analyze the emotional and behavioral characteristics of individuals, groups, or activities. A *psychoanalyst* can be a psychologist or a psychiatrist. A psychoanalyst must have a degree in psychology or psychiatry, the former being at least a master's and preferably a doctorate. A psychoanalyst, if he is a psychiatrist, has a medical degree. If he is a psychologist, he will have a minimum of a master's degree, but he is not a medical doctor.

Q. "I recently read an ad for an ointment said to be good for *rash, eczema,* and *dermatitis.* Am I crazy, or aren't they all the same?"
A. You're not crazy. The ad agency simply went to a thesaurus and used synonyms to make the product appear to cure more than one thing. *Rash, eczema,* and *dermatitis* are all the same thing. (So are hives, urticaria, exanthema, and uredo.)

Q. "Why did my professor call *Pygmalion* a '*Shavian*' comedy? Shouldn't he have said, 'Shaw-ian'?"
A. *Shavian* comes from "Shavius", a Latin form for the name Shaw. Therefore, your instructor was perfectly correct when he spoke of one of George Bernard Shaw's plays as Shavian. We also speak of a person's wit or sense of humor as being Shavian, meaning simply that the humor is like George Bernard Shaw's—dry, barbed, and very clever. GBS, himself, coined Shavian to describe his works. He originally called them Shaw-ian, but that was awkward. So, old GBS, who was *never* awkward, switched to Latin.

Q. "Most *slang* words seem to originate with teenagers. What do educated people think of slang?"

A. I'm an educated person. And I feel that slang is a very colorful and necessary component of a growing language when used sparingly and judiciously. I don't believe that slang should be used in an academic atmosphere, in a job situation, or when trying to communicate vital information which requires clear, specific, formal English. However, I love the word "gross" to describe something immensely negative, and I feel that "humongous" says so much. Another coined word, this one by Levi's (the jean people) advertising agency, is *skosh*—meaning a trifle large or smaller. It has a lovely sound and has a Japanese etymology. And it may make it into our language as a permanent fixture.

Q. "What is the meaning of *tachistoscopic?*"
A. The term originated during World War II, when it was discovered that many of our gunners were shooting down American planes instead of enemy planes, since they reacted to the stimulus of a dot in the sky as the enemy. A device was perfected which, when attached to a film projector, would allow the user to flash on a screen silhouettes of airplanes, thus enabling the viewer to quickly identify those silhouettes as friend or foe. Today, in America, this kind of equipment will be found in some airline training schools where pilots must look at a dozen gauges quickly, or in reading training programs where students are taught to read groups of words at one time.
It is forbidden to use tachistoscopic devices in advertising. Some years ago, in the midwest, a tachistoscopic device was used to flash "POP-CORN" on the movie screen subliminally. A near-riot of popcorn-lovers is alleged to have ensued. The origin of the word lies in the Greek *takhistos* meaning "most swift" and *scope* meaning "to see."

Q. "What does *tomentose* mean? Spiro Agnew used it several times in a speech at our college campus. In the news coverage of the speech, it was reported that there was a near-riot when he used the term."
A. The word comes from the Latin *tomentum*, a stuffing of hair, and today it means "covered with long, matted hair." So what Mr. Agnew was really doing was calling his audience a bunch of hairy apes. Why he used this word is a little beyond me; perhaps he wished to insult them without their knowledge. But many did catch on.

Q. "Will you spell out the difference between *tortuous* and *tortu-rous?*

A. Happy to. *Tortuous* is an adjective meaning "full of twists, wind-ing, or crooked." *Torturous* is an adjective which means "cruel, in-flicting pain."

Prefixes, Roots, and Suffixes

Q. "What is the difference between *dis*interested and *un*interested?"
A. The prefix *dis* means "apart from." Someone who is *dis*interested is indifferent: free of bias and self-interest, impartial. *Un*interested means definitely *not* interested because the prefix *un* means "not." A person who is disinterested would make a good arbiter in a dispute since he or she has no personal reason to favor one side over the other. Someone uninterested, on the other hand, wouldn't care whether the dispute was settled at all.

Q. "My doctor said he has to give me a *subcutaneous* injection next week. Is that something I should fear?"
A. Your question illustrates why it can be important to have a knowledge of prefixes, roots, and suffixes. *Sub* merely means "under or below" (submarine, subtle, subtraction, subsist); *cutaneous* means "skin." Your doctor merely wants to give you a shot. Perhaps you would like to know the derivation of some other common medical prefixes and suffixes.

ARTERIO-   (artery): *arteriosclerosis*, hardening of the arteries; *arteriospasm*, spasm of an artery; *arteritis*, inflammation of an artery.

ARTHRO-	(joints): *arthritis*, inflammation of the joints; *arthrocele*, swelling of the joints.
-ECTOMY	(surgical removal): *appendectomy*, removal of the appendix; *gastrectomy*, removal of the stomach; *hysterectomy*, removal of the uterus.
-EMIA	(blood): *anemia*, a deficiency in the blood; *leukemia*, a blood disease; *hyperemia*, excess blood in a body part.
INTRA-	(within): *intranasal*, within the nose; *intracranial*, within the cranium, or head; *intraduodenum*, within the duodenum.
-ITIS	(inflammation): *dermatitis*, inflammation of the skin; *carditis*, inflammation of the heart; *trichitis*, inflammation of the scalp.
-MANIA	(violent desire): *pyromania*, a desire to start fires; *phagomania*, a desire to eat; *hypermania*, excessively manic state.
MYO-	(muscle): *myocardial*, relating to heart muscle; *myodystrophy*, malnourished muscle; *myoclonus*, muscle spasms.
NEURO-	(nerve): *neuritis*, inflammation of a nerve; *neurocardiac*, nerve of the heart; *neurocyctes*, nerve cells.
-OMA	(tumor): *nephroma*, tumor of the kidney; *hepatoma*, tumor of the liver; *hemangioma*, tumor made up of blood.
-OPIA	(defect of eye): *myopia*, short-sightedness; *dysopia*, defective vision; *exotropia*, defective eye movement.
ORTHO-	(straightening, correction): *orthopedics*, correction of skeletal deformities; *orthodontics*, straightening of teeth; *orthopsychiatry*, correction of a mental illness.
-OSIS	(diseased state, process): *neurosis*, a nervous disorder; *psychosis*, a state of mental disorder; *miosis*, disease of the eye pupil.
OSTEO-	(bone): *osteoma*, tumor of the bone; *osteoscope*, pain in the bone; *osteopathy*, disease of the bone.

-PATHY	(disease): *neuropathy,* disease of the nervous system; *psychopathy,* extreme mental disorder; *gastropathy,* disease of the stomach.
PHOBIA	(fear): *hydrophobia,* a fear of water; *acrophobia,* fear of high places; *hodophobia,* a fear of travel.
-PLASTY	(repair): *colpoplasty,* repair of the vagina; *mastoplasty,* repair of the breast; *metroplasty,* repair of the uterus.
PROCTO-	(rectum): *proctologist,* specialist in rectal diseases; *proctitis,* inflammation of the rectum; *proctectomy,* excision of the rectum.
PSYCHO-	(mind): *psychosis,* a morbid state of mind; *psychology,* the study of the mind; *psychiatrist,* specialist in mental illness.
SCLERO-	(hardening): *sclerosis,* the process of hardening; *sclerodermatitis,* inflammatory hardening of the skin; *scleroid,* hard texture.
THERAPY	(treatment): *psychotherapy,* treatment of the mind; *radiotherapy,* treatment by x-ray; *hydrotherapy,* treatment by water.
THROMBO-	(blood clot): *thrombectomy,* removal of a blood clot; *thromboid,* resembling a clot; *thrombogenic,* formation of a clot.
-TROPHY	(atrophy): *dystrophy,* faulty nutrition; *abiotrophy,* loss of vitality of cells.

Q. "I am familiar with some prefixes, such as *un* for 'not' and *pro* for 'for.' Where can I find a list of others?"

A. Right here! Many prefixes, suffixes, and roots have come to us from Latin or Greek. Once you become interested and fascinated by them, your knowledge of English will undergo a very rapid and seemingly magical expansion. You will find yourself analyzing words, understanding new words almost instantly, gaining new insight into, and recognizing subtle shades of meaning in, familiar words: demise, for example. The common understanding of *demise* is that it means "death," or "to die." (It has a secondary meaning, "to transfer an estate by will or lease," but this meaning need not concern us now). I chose the word "demise" to illustrate the new insight you will gain into common words once you have a nodding acquaintance with prefixes, roots, and suffixes.

The prefix *de* means "away, down, from, or of," and the root *mise* means "send." Put the two together and you have "send away," or "die".

Here's another. The prefix *mal* means "bad," and I am sure you can think of many words where this applies: malice, malign, malignancy, malevolence, and so on. There's also *malediction,* a wonderful word which, translated, literally means "to speak ill" and whose dictionary definition is "to curse." We can change this word instantly just by giving it a different prefix. Let's choose the prefix *"bene"* which means "good" and join it to "diction" (from the Latin *dicere* = "to say.") The word quickly becomes *benediction*—"a blessing, or the act of blessing."

Here's a list of some of the more common prefixes. They will enrich your state of words and your knowledge of your language.

COMMON LATIN PREFIXES

Meaning: to, toward

A	ascend, aspire, ascribe
AC	accede, accord, accrue, accumulate
AD	adhere, admit, advertisement
AF	affect, affix, affiance
AG	aggravate, aggregate
AL	allot, allusion, allocate
AN	announce, annex
AP	apparent, appendage, applaud
AR	arrive, arraign
AS	assign, assist
AT	attend, attest

Meaning: both, around

AMBI	ambidexterous, ambivalent

Meaning: before

ANTE	antechamber, antecedent

Meaning: together, with

COG	cognate, cogent, cogitate
COL	college, collateral
COM	commerce, communal, committee
CON	configuration, context
COR	correlate, corrosion

Meaning: from, down

DE	decline, devious, detritus

Meaning: out, from, away

E	evoke, event, elongate
EF	effect, efficacious
EX	expatriate, extrinsic, exigency

NOTE:"Ex" is also used with a noun to indicate "former" = ex-president, ex-wife, ex-landlord.

COMMON GREEK PREFIXES

Meaning: not, without

A	apolitical, atheist, asexual
AN	anarchy, anomaly, anathema

Meaning: against

ANTI	anti-social

Meaning: away, off

APO	apostle, apology, apocryphal

Meaning: upon, beside

EP	epode, epoch
EPH	ephemeral
EPI	epidermis, epithet, episode

Meaning: beside

PARA	paragraph, paraphrase, parallel

Meaning: with, together

SYN	synonymous, synopsis, synagogue
SYM	sympathy, symphony, symmetry
SYL	syllogism, syllable

Roots are the body of a word. Words live in families. Once you know that *cred* is the root for "belief, trust," you can instantly recognize a whole host of words: credible, credence, incredible, credibility, credulous. Here are some common roots.

COMMON LATIN ROOTS

Meaning: take, hold

CAP	captious, capable, captivate
CEPT	precept, deception, inception
CIP	anticipate, recipient, incipient

Meaning: make, do

FAC	fact, factor, factotum
FECT	disaffection, affect, defective
FIC	efficacy, edifice

Meaning: carry, bring, bear

FER	confer, infer, proffer

Meaning: end, limit

FIN	define, infinitive, final

Meaning: send, throw

MISE	demise, surmise, promise
MISS	missive, missile, submission
MIT	commit, omit, permit

Meaning: rule, straighten, arrange

RECT	erect, direct, rector
REG	reign, regiment, regime
RESS	dress, redress, address
RIG	incorrigible, rigid

Meaning: stand

SIST	desist, persist, subsist
STA	stable, stanza, stanchion
STAT	statue, statute, static

COMMON GREEK ROOTS

Meaning: man

ANTHROP   anthropology, misanthrope, philanthropic

Meaning: self

AUTO   automobile, autobiography, autopsy

Meaning: life

BIO   biography, biotic, biology

Meaning: write

GRAPH   autograph, stenography, bibliography

Meaning: different

HETERO   heterosexual, heterogeneous

Meaning: the same

HOMO   homosexual, homonym, homogenized

Meaning: word, speech, science

LOG   logic, prologue, epilogue

Meaning: loving, friendly, kind

PHIL   philosopher, Philadelphia, philharmonic

Now you can successfully join some prefixes to roots to form words. You know the root *graph* means "write" and the prefix *epi* means "upon" so you can correctly join them to form *epigraph* which means "something written at the start of a book, chapter, or poem." But there's more. Even though you are successfully joining prefixes to roots, you still have to add suffixes in order to gain maximum word power.

COMMON SUFFIXES AND THEIR MEANINGS

Meaning: state of, act of, quality of

-ACY   celibacy, piracy, delicacy

Meaning: state of, act of, quality of

-ANCY,
-ENCY   buoyancy, brilliancy, agency

Meaning: state of, act of, quality of

-ANCE,
-ENCE   severance, sustenance, diligence

Meaning: resembling, full of, pertaining to

-IVE   restive, native, secretive

Meaning: to make, to do

-IZE   dramatize, customize, maximize

Meaning: possessing, having or full of

-OUS   fatuous, delicious, ambitious

Meaning: one who does

-ANT   defendant, attendant, tenant

Meaning: Quality of, State of

-ACITY   capacity, tenacity, veracity

Meaning: quality of

-TUDE   exactitude, magnitude

V

Spelling Tricks
and Demons

We feel compelled to include a chapter about spelling. It's going to help you, but there isn't anything or anyone in this world who can transform you into a master or mistress of spelling in this language. If you assiduously read and absorb all of the material that we have included, you will be better off than before you began. But only if our language were radically transformed, into a totally phonetic communications system, would it be possible for anyone to be able to spell every word in it.

What do I mean by phonetic and unphonetic? *Phonetics* studies the relationship between the letters in our words and the sounds that these letters make. If our language were phonetic, then each letter would have only one sound, regardless of where it was placed in a given word. In our unphonetic language, many letters are pronounced differently from word to word; sometimes they have no sounds at all. We have twenty-six letters in our alphabet. Ideally, there should be one letter for each sound.

There are just a few books printed in ITA, the Initial Teaching Alphabet, in which each letter possesses only one sound, so it is quite simple not only to spell words but also to read them. I have seen tiny children in elementary school, taught via the ITA alphabet, reading five and six syllable words with no effort at all. Unfortunately, very few books have been printed in ITA, so that it becomes absolutely mandatory that we include this chapter in our book.

In the year 1755, Dr. Samuel Johnson published the first great English dictionary. He is responsible for a great many of the inconsistencies in spelling that irritate us today. Dr. Johnson, perhaps because he had respect for Latin words from which many English words derived, added a Latin touch to many words; he is responsible for inserting a *b* in *debt*, because there was a *b* in the Latin word from which it came *(debitum)*; for the same reason, he put a *p* in *receipt*, although he neglected to put one in *"conceit"* (Middle English *conceite*) and *"deceit"* (Middle English *deceite*).

In America, both Benjamin Franklin and Noah Webster rebelled against illogical spelling, and suggested reforms and simplifications. Franklin wanted to omit all unnecessary letters, suggesting *bred* for bread, *giv* for give, *kee* for key, *tuf* for tough, *blud* for blood, and so on. Webster suggested *wimmen* for women and *tung* for tongue. Nothing much came of these movements. But when Webster finally published his dictionary, which has long been the standard authority for American English, he changed many words from British to American spelling: jail for gaol, glamor for glamour, honor instead of honour, wagon for waggon, and jewelry for jewellry.

Usage determines English language rules, ultimately, except in spelling. So you might as well learn *to get it right,* as Thomas Hardy did. Someone once told Hardy that *sugar* was the only word in the English language where *su* was pronounced "shŏo" Hardy said, "Are you sure?"

Before we begin, here's a suggestion. Have you ever tried to look up a word you couldn't spell in the dictionary? It's not easy, but it would certainly be helpful if you could. So, go to your local bookstore and buy a small volume entitled *Webster's New World Misspeller's Dictionary* (Simon & Schuster, 1983). Why? Because it contains words commonly misspelled according to *how* they are misspelled. Here's an example. Suppose you think that floccinaucinihilipilification should be spelled flaccinaucinihilipilification. All you do is look it up, alphabetically listed, under flaccinaucinihilipilification, and, lo and behold, ods bodkins, what do you find? Next to flaccinaucinihilipilification, you find the correct spelling: floccinaucinihilipilification. No meanings, just the right spelling. Then you go to the regular dictionary to get the other information. Useful, eh? But we'll still try to spell everything in the following discussion correctly.

Q. "Is there more than one English alphabet?"

A. The alphabet you learned in school was simply and purely the *names* of the letters we use to make our words; it did not, for the most part contain the *sounds* that the letters made. So the answer to your question is yes, most emphatically; we have two English alphabets, the one simply giving the names of the letters and the one made up of the actual sounds of the letters. Here is the phonetic alphabet as you should have learned it:

a as in c*a*t

a as in c*a*re

a as in c*a*r

b as in *buh*

c as in *c*ar

c as in ra*c*e

d as in *d*ug

e as in *e*at

e as in l*e*t

e as in h*e*r

f as in *f*antastic

g as in *g*irl

g as in ra*g*e

h as in *h*at

i as in h*i*t

i as in wr*i*te

j as in *j*et

k as in *k*it

l as in *l*ight

m as in *m*arvelous

n as in *n*ew

o as in lope

o as in c*o*t

p as in *p*en

qu as in *qu*ick

r as in *r*ight

s as in *s*tupendous

t as in *t*errific

u as in c*u*re

u as in *u*p

v as in *v*ictory

w as in *w*in

x as in *x*-ray

y as in *y*ellow

y as in mone*y*

z as in la*z*y

And then there are the consonant combinations.

bl-	blue	sh-	shy
br-	brown	sk-	skin
cl-	clear	sl-	sleep
cr-	crown	sm-	small
dr-	drink	sn-	snow
fl-	fly	sp-	sport
fr-	fry	st-	star
gl-	glide	sw-	swim
gr-	green	th-	thin
pl-	plan	tr-	tree
pr-	proud	tw-	twin

Q. "I have a very old dictionary. Should I buy a new one?"
A. If your dictionary is outdated, and contains words no longer used while lacking current words, it is time for a replacement. The actual title really doesn't matter. That's just a personal choice; different people like different dictionaries for different reasons. You are going to have to decide whether you want an abridged or an unabridged dictionary. (See the bibliography.) Don't even consider the little paperback dictionaries. They will only be frustrating, as they contain so few words. For between $60 and $80, you can purchase a large unabridged dictionary containing hundreds of thousands of words plus valuable additional information: a history of the English language, guides to pronunciation, a biographical dictionary, a chronological list of presidents, a section on business mathematics, tables of flags, special sections on foreign words and phrases, and so many more sections of genuine practical use that it would take too much space to list them all. Suffice it to say that an unabridged dictionary is an invaluable possession.

Its only real drawback is that it is really heavy (not to say impossible) to carry about from place to place. A good hardcover abridged dictionary usually has a hundred and fifty thousand or so of the most commonly used words. Additionally, it provides the etymology or history of each word, the part of speech for each word, and usage information for some words. You will usually spend $10 to $12 for an abridged dictionary; it is easier to carry about but obviously has fewer words and less information.

For each entry, the following information will be listed:

The language from which the word derived

L	Latin
Gk	Greek
E	English
OE	Old English
FR	French
GMC	Germanic

The part of speech to which the word belongs

n	noun
v	verb
adj	adjective
adv	adverb
conj	conjunction
inter	interjection

Word usage

sl	slang
col	colloquial
obs	obsolete, no longer used
illit	illiterate, not used by the educated

Q. "Can you tell me how to use a dictionary?"

A. At the tops of all the pages in a dictionary you will locate two words, one on the left, one on the right. These are called *guide words*. The one on the left is the first word on that page; the one on the right is the last word on the page. So when looking for any word, simply look at the guide words to see whether the word you need to locate is on their page.

At the bottom of every page you will find a pronunciation key. It will look something like this:

ă pat/ā pay/âr care/ä father/b bib/ch church/d deed/ĕ pet/ē be/f fife/g
gag/h hat/hw which/ĭ pit/ī pie/îr pier/j judge/k kick/l lid, needle/m
mum/n no, sudden/ng thing/ŏ pot/ō toe/ô paw, for/oi noise/ou out/o͝o
took/o͞o boot/p pop/r roar/s sauce/sh ship, dish

t tight/th thin, path/th this, bathe/ŭ cut/ûr urge/v valve/w with/y
yes/z zebra, size/zh vision/ə about, item, edible, gallop, circus/

I think you can figure out why this key is on every page. If, for
instance, you wish to pronounce a word spelled phonetically with an
a with two dots over it, just look at the bottom of the page and find
that *ä*: next to it will probably be the word father, illustrating the
correct pronunciation. You would be amazed how many students
come to me with words on paper asking how they are pronounced.
After I show them how to use pronunciation keys their problem
disappears.

It is important to be able to read phonetic spellings in the dictionary because the phonetic spelling tells you how to pronounce the
word. Here is a simplified pronunciation guide telling you how to
use the phonetic spellings in your dictionary

Next to the original listing of the word is another spelling. This
is what we call phonetic spelling. It is spelled according to how it is
pronounced. Above vowels, or vowel groups, ei, ea, ai, etc., you will
find little marks which are called "diacritical" marks. These marks
simply tell you the sounds of the vowel. Now, observe carefully. If
you go to the bottom of the page in your dictionary, you will find a
list of words each with a vowel marked in a specific way. If you find
a word with an "a," for instance, marked thusly: a, and it's the word
cake, then, you know that "a" in your word in pronounced the same
way if it, too, has a straight line over it: *cake*. This straight line is
called a macron, similar to the cookie named macaroon, and it indicates what we call a l-o-n-n-g sound, meaning that the sound travels
the full length of the speech-making tract from voice box past your
tongue out through your lips.

We also have other A sounds: Any sound that is not long is called
short. By "short," we simply mean that the vowel sound starts in the
voice box and travels only a short distance. In words such as *cat, bar,*

the "A" would be marked in your dictionary in a variety of ways because different dictionaries use different marks. They all fall into the general category of what we call "breves."

Different dictionaries mark their vowels "short" in different ways. Some will put the little half circle upside down over the vowel (a). Others will put a single dot over the vowel (a) and still others will not put anything over the vowel, assuming that *you* know the meaning of the absence of a diacritical mark. They take so much for granted. Consult your own dictionary and discover its method. And, if in doubt, call me.

This information will also apply to the rest of your vowels. You should also know what a dieresis is. A dieresis ¨ placed over the second of two adjacent vowels indicates that the two vowels are pronounced separately in a word. In the word "dieresis," for instance, the "e" is pronounced as a separate vowel. Have you ever seen an upside down "e" and wondered whether it was a typographical error? Well, it wasn't. It's called a *schwa*.

What does it mean?

It stands for an unaccented short vowel sound. Let's take the word "doctor." If it were spelled phonetically, it would look like this: D Ŏ K T əR. Notice that the first O has a *breve* over it. And the second O has been replaced by a *schwa*.

What does it mean?

Simply put, the first O is pronounced more loudly than the second one. the second O is pronounced quietly, and it's short.

Please familiarize yourselves with this information. And, if you have any questions, CALL ME. You know the number, and, if you don't, here it is again. (805) 378-1494, just in case you have any questions about the long and short of it.

If you have trouble finding a word, remember the sound of it doesn't necessarily help much with the spelling. Here is a table of possible alternatives.

If you think a word is spelled with:

ac—try k, qu, or s	j–try g or dg
f–try ph or v	k–try c or qu
g–try j or dg	qu–try k or c

s–try ps, c, z, ch, or sh

v–try f or ph

x–try s, sh, sc, x, or ew

ly–try i or e

z–try s, sh, sc, x, or ew

ew–try eu or oo

oo–try u, ew, eu, ue or eau

shun–try tion or sion

sh–try ch, ti, si or se

ch–try sh or tch

el–try le

tch–try ch

per–try pre or pur

pre–try per or pur

pur–try pre or per

Q. "What are the different letter categories?"

A. We have two categories of letters in our language: consonants and vowels. The vowels are a, e, i, o, and u, and sometimes the letter y. All of the other letters are consonants.

Now, here are what I consider to be the salient principles of phonetics. I hope you know them already, but I think they will represent new material to most readers. They are not in any special order, and I have eliminated those which have only limited application and those to which there are so many exceptions that the rule is hardly worth learning. There are *some* exceptions for most of them, but this has to be expected and accepted.

1. When two vowels are together in a word, the first one is sounded, and the second one is silent: *feed, read, receipt*. Lead (in a pencil) is an exception, as is I read the book yesterday.

2. An *e* at the end of a word containing a vowel before the final consonant makes the vowel say its own name: *rate, cede, came*.

3. In some words *gh* is silent; in others, it has the sound of *f: straight, sight, enough, laugh*.

4. When *c* and *h* are together, the sound is like that heard in *chime*. When there is a *t* before the *ch*, the *t* is silent: *watch*.

5. When *a* is followed by *u, w,* or *l,* it usually has the *au* sound: *caught, raw, call*.

6. In words of one syllable with two vowels at the end, the first vowel is long and the second one is silent: *bee, sea, lie*.

7. If a word ends in *s, ss, sh, ch,* or *x,* always add *es* to make the plural; in all other words, add only *s: gases, lasses, rashes, batches, mixes; runs, plays*.

8. When *x* is at the beginning of a word, it has the sound of *z: xylophone*.

9. When there is a consonant before the final *y* in a word, the *y* is usually changed to *i* before adding *es: body/bodies, carry/carries*.

10. When adding *ing* to a word ending in *y*, keep the *y* before the *ing: tarrying, worrying*.

11. If a word ends in silent *e*, keep the *e* before the suffixes *ly* and *ness: homely, sameness*.

12. Before *ure*, a single *s* or *z* is pronounced *zh: pleasure, seizure, measure*.

13. The letter *g* before *a, o,* or *u* is hard: *got, gaff, gut*.

14. The letter *g* before *e, i,* or *y* is soft: *gypsy, gyration, ginger, gem*.

15. The same rules apply to the letter *c*. *C* before an *a, o,* or *u* is hard: *cat, cot, cut*.

16. But *c* before *e, i,* or *y* is soft: *race, city, racy*.

17. Double consonants in a word usually have a short vowel sound before them: *dimming, kissing*. Most words double their final consonant before a suffix beginning with a vowel: *hop/hopping/hopper; tip/tipping/tipper*.

18. A single consonant before a suffix beginning with a vowel usually indicates a long vowel sound before the single consonant: *oration, raving*.

19. The *sh* sound may be spelled in many ways. Here are just a few:

> sh (rash) ti (nutrition)
> ce (ocean) ci (delicious)
> ch (machine) s (sure)

20. The letter *p* is silent when directly followed by an *s: psalm*.

21. When *y* is the only vowel in two- or three-letter words it has the sound of a long *i: cry, dry*.

22. When double *c* occurs in a word and the second *c* has the sound of *s*, the first *c* has the sound of *k: accent, accident, flaccid*.

23. In plurals of words ending in *f*, the *f* changes into *v: halves, knives*.

24. When a single vowel is between two consonants, it is usually short: *hat, cot, fit*.

There are more phonetic rules. We felt that the preceding ones are the most important, and will provide a feeling of confidence when you attempt to analyze and pronounce words. Naturally, we still have problems: catsup/ketchup, victuals/vittles, tough-trough-thorough-though-through, pronounce-pronunciation in which the spelling and pronunciation leave much to be desired.

Phonetics is directly related to spelling. However, a knowledge of phonetics will give you insight into only a fraction of the words we use each day. Perhaps that may be why so many of us possess limited vocabularies, and why so many daily newspapers are written on a sixth-grade vocabulary level, and why so many college textbooks have been recalled.

Many educational establishments in the United States, at least at this time, have surrendered and accepted the "fact" that many of us will never raise our sights above our present level. We are not of that mind. We have always believed that "Today is the first day of the rest of our lives." And I want you to believe in this motto too. We have had tens of thousands of clients, private and in classrooms, who have approached us with the statement, "I'm really kind of stupid; I don't have much of an education. Do you think there's a chance for me to start learning at this stage in my life?" And you should see them a few months later! My heavens, ods bodkins, and all that: they know more than we do!

Q. "I need a lot of spelling demons to practice. Can you send me some?"

A. Here is a horde of spelling demons. Rules don't apply to them. You simply have to learn them by heart.

abbreviate	absence	accidentally
accumulate	achieve	acquaintance
admittance	advertisement	aerial
aggressive	aisle	allowance
all right	amateur	analysis
analyze	anecdote	anniversary
anonymous	anxiety	appearance
argument	athletic	attendance
awkward	banquet	barrel
behavior	believe	benefit
bicycle	bookkeeper	bulletin
bureau	business	calendar
capital	capitol	captain

career	category	cemetery
changeable	chauffeur	clothes
colonel	column	committee
competitor	concede	condemn
conscience	conscientious	conscious
contemporary	continuous	convenience
coolly	cordially	correspondence
counterfeit	courageous	courtesy
criticism	criticize	curiosity
curious	deceive	defendant
efficient	delinquent	desert
despair	desperate	dessert
development	dining	disappear
disappoint	disastrous	dissatisfied
distinction	distinguish	doubt
efficient	eighth	eligible
embarrass	emergency	envelope
environment	equipped	exaggerate
exceed	exercise	existence
explanation	extraordinary	familiar
February	foreign	grammar
handkerchief	hygiene	immigrant
independence	inflammable	interfere
knowledge	laboratory	lawyer
library	license	lieutenant
lightning	loneliness	maintenance
mathematics	meanness	mediocre
mileage	millionaire	misspell
naturally	necessary	neighbor
ninety	nuisance	occasion
occasionally	occur	occurred
omitted	opinion	pamphlet
parallel	paralyze	particularly
permanent	permissible	personally
perspiration	physician	possess
possession	prairie	precede
preferable	preparation .	privilege
probably	procedure	proceed
pronunciation	psychology	really
recede	receipt	recommend

reference	rehearse	religious
repetition	restaurant	rhythm
ridiculous	sacrilegious	scissors
secretary	separate	sergeant
similar	sincerely	sophomore
souvenir	spaghetti	straight
substitute	succeed	superintendent
supersede	surprise	suspicious
syllable	technique	temperament
temperature	temporary	thorough
tomatoes	tomorrow	tragedy
truly	unforgettable	unnecessary
vacuum	vegetable	villain
Wednesday	weird	whether

Now, to become a better speller, you should know your phonetics rules. Then there are some basic rules of spelling. They do work, and you'll encounter them right here in this chapter. Then there are some shortcuts, some tricks. I'm sure you know some that I don't know. If you do, send them to me (or to the publisher, who will forward them directly to my office). As for those demon words, which do not adhere to the rules and which simply must be memorized, try the chapter on study skills: you will find some suggestions about your memory and how to use it.

1. In contractions, you always place the apostrophe where there was missing letter. So, *did not* becomes *didn't*, *would not* becomes *wouldn't; it is* becomes *it's*. But never use an apostrophe in a possessive pronoun (his, her, yours, its, theirs, ours, whose).
2. Oh, this is a juicy one. I hope that you already know it. Only one verb in English ends in *sede: supersede*.
3. Only three verbs end in *ceed: succeed, proceed, exceed*. There's a way to remember this one. Look at the first letters of the three verbs: *s p e*, the first three letters of the word SPELL.
4. All other verbs with this final sound *(seed)* end in *cede: recede, precede*.
5. In a one-syllable word, double the final consonant before a suffix starting with a vowel: *hog/hoggish*.

6. If the final consonant comes after two vowels, do not double the final consonant: *reap/reaping, clear/cleared*.

7. If the final consonant comes after another consonant, don't double it: *thirst/thirstier, trust/trusted*.

8. Here's a rule with some exceptions, which will follow directly. If you have a word of two or more syllables before a suffix starting with a vowel, double the final consonant only if it is an accented syllable: *admit/admitted, commit/committee*.

9. There are three exceptions to Rule 8. If the accent moves back to the first syllable after you add the suffix, do not double the final consonant. *Prefer/preference;* BUT *prefer/preferring*. Do you understand? In preferring, the accent stayed on the *fer*, so we still doubled that final *r*. But in preference, the accent shifted back to *pre*. Therefore, we did not double the *r* before the suffix.

10. Exception number 2 to Rule 8: If the final consonant comes after another consonant, don't double that final consonant: *respond/responded*.

11. Exception number 3 to Rule 8: If the final consonant comes after two vowels, do not double the final consonants: *repeat/repeated*.

12. If you wish to add a suffix beginning with a vowel to any word ending in *e*, drop the *e* and add the suffix: *relate/relating*.

13. But, with words ending in *ce* or *ge*, if you wish to add suffixes beginning in *a* or *o*, keep the final *e*: *brace/braceable, courage/courageous*.

14. There are some exceptions to the above rule: *dye/dyeing, be/being*.

15. To add a suffix beginning with a consonant to any word ending in *e*, do not drop the final *e*; just add the suffix.

16. BUT, there are exceptions: *true/truly; awe/awful; argue/argument; judge/judgment; acknowledge/acknowledgment*.

17. When a prefix is added to a word, the word's spelling stays the same: *dissimilar, reenter*.

18. Only the most important word in a compound takes *s* or *es* when it becomes plural: *mother-in-law/mothers-in-law*.

19. If you have a word of two or more syllables, convict´ , double the final consonants, only if it has an accented syllable, before a suffix starting with a vowel. So, we have the word re spect´ ; it is accented on the second syllable: spect´ .

20. To form the plural ending in *s, ss, x, z, sh,* or *ch*, simply add *es: sexes, fishes, passes*.

21. To form the plural of a word ending in *y* after a vowel, add *s:* *relay/relays*.
22. To form the plural of a word ending in *y* after a consonant, add *es* after changing the *y* to *i: baby/babies, city/cities*.
23. To pluralize a word ending in *o* after a consonant, add *es: potato/potatoes*.
24. To pluralize a word ending in *o* after a vowel, add only *s: stereo/stereos*.
25. Then comes perhaps the most widely known spelling rule: Put *i* before *e* except after *c* or when it's sounded like *ā*, as in *eighty* and *weigh*. *Eighty* and *weigh* have the sound of *ā* while *achieve* and *priest*, for example, have the sound of *ē*.
26. There are notable exceptions to the above rule. They are: *sheik, seize, counterfeit, weird, height, sufficient, deficient, ancient, science, either, ancient*.

There are more than twenty-seven spelling rules. But I have endeavored to present the most important ones. Those you know, skip over. Those you don't know, learn, please. It will really help, in what you know, and what impression you make on others.

Now, here are some tricks of the trade: shortcuts designed to help you remember some oddly-spelled words. These are only a few. You can design your own spelling demons.

I have already given you the one about *succeed, proceed, exceed*. In *separate* and *comparative*, look for a *rat* in both words.

Coolly: You can spell cool; just add the *ly*.

Superintendent: Most people make the mistake of spelling it superintendant; you can easily avoid this pitfall if you think of the superintendent collecting the rent/dent; got it?

Stationary: Means standing; remember the *a* in stand.

Stationery: Means paper goods; remember the *e* in paper.

Principal: This is an old one: My *pal* is the princi*pal*.

All right: Should not be written alright, which is substandard. Just remember that it is the opposite of *all wrong*.

Conscience: Is simply con + science.

The list could go on and on. Now you can start your own list.

Q. "What is the smallest number of letters in a syllable, and what is the smallest number of syllables that a word can have?"

A. The answer to the first question is . . . one. A one-letter word is also a one-syllable word. Of course, we do have silent vowels in words. Most final *e*'s are silent and belong with the syllable preceding the final e: retrace: the final e is part of the second syllable: trace, so, if you were writing this word at the end of a line, you would never break the word except between the two syllables: re trace; you couldn't do this: retr ace.

Q. "I'm never really sure how to divide a word at the end of a line. Can you give me any help?"

A. One rule to remember is that when two consonants are between two vowels, you always make the break between the two consonants: *let-ter, fas-ter*. When a single consonant appears between two vowels, it is usually part of the syllable that follows: *i-deal, e-qual*. Syllabification is very important, too, when you are confused about how to pronounce a word. If you are aware of its spelling and correct syllabic breaks, the pronunciation becomes that much easier: How do you pronounce February? Athlete? Veterinarian? Well, let's see by breaking each one down by syllables: ath lete; many careless speakers say "ath e lete." That's not how it is spelled; therefore, we can't arbitrarily put that extra middle "e'" in. What about the second word? Feb ru a ry. See the "r" in the second syllable? Well, you just can't leave it out and say "Feb u ary." That "r" has a proud place in that month, and it simply can't be idly disregarded. And the third word: vet er i na ri an. You can't say vetrinarian. What happened to the "e" just before "r"? It worked hard to get in there. We can't discard it like an old shoe.

Another important rule is: when two vowels are together, they are usually divided to make separate syllables, except when they combine to make a single sound: *re-cre-ate, vi-a, ar-e-a;* but, *lei-sure, fea-si-ble, read*.

Q. "Can you provide a list of often-confused words?"

A. The list that follows contains some common homonyms and look-alikes.

I accept that gift.
Except for him, we will all go.

There is an addition to my house.
This is the first edition of the book.

This will affect you greatly.
The effect was incredible.

Are you all ready?
We are already there.

We are all together.
Altogether, there are twelve women.

He made an allusion to his stay in the desert.
We saw an illusion in the desert.

The minister stood next to the altar.
Will you alter your plans?

The tent was made from canvas.
We will canvass all the houses in the neighborhood.

Washington is the capital of the country.
How much capital do you have to invest
There is the capitol building.

Did you buy many clothes?
We washed the car with some old cloths.

We finished the first course of the meal.
The sandpaper was very coarse.

This tie complements the rest of that outfit.
She paid me a nice compliment.

Will you counsel me?
You can renew your passport at the consul's office.
There was a long debate in the city council.

He deserted his animals.
The desert was hot.
We had ice cream for dessert.

She is a very decent person.
He always dissents.
Their descent from the mountain-top was difficult.

The car had dual headlights.
They fought a duel.

He is an eminent attorney.
We are in imminent danger.

We were formally introduced.
Formerly, she was an astronaut.

Go forth into the word.
He is their fourth son.

The gilt of the picture frame shone in the firelight.
Guilt was written all over his face.

Did you hear what they said?
Here it is.

What an ingenious invention!
They're too ingenuous to understand your sarcasm.

Later, we will go to Disneyland.
If the choice were between Bob and Mary, I'd vote for the latter.

The lead is in the pencil.
Lead the way!
We led them yesterday.

The tiger got out of the cage and is loose.
Did you lose your keys?

We passed the lake in our walk.
It is three minutes past ten.

Finally we had peace.
Give me a piece of pie, please.

I have a personal problem.
Do you work in the personnel department?

The plane ride was very smooth.
It's as plain as the nose on your face.

George Washington preceded John Adams as President.
They proceeded down the path.

The principal is the head of the school.
That is a matter of principle.

Be quiet!
She is a quite a person.

He respectfully declined the offer.
They are three and four years old respectively.

That is a beautiful rite to observe.
Did you write your letter?

We visited the building site.
Will you cite an example?
What a sight to behold!

What is the status of women?
The statute was observed by all.

Then we went to the movies.
He is better than I am.

These are their shoes.
There they go.
They're good people.

He threw the ball.
They ran through the tunnel.

He went to school.
They are too much!
We have two cars.

The weather is fine.
Whether or not he does it is not important.

Whose book is this?

Who's going to the movies?

You're a fine person.
These are your books.

Q. "How can I improve my knowledge of pronunciation?"
A. There are really only two methods of developing this skill. One is the look-say method and the other, a thorough knowledge of phonetic rules. The look-say method really never stops; it is an approach requiring the learner to look at a word, learn how it is pronounced, and then use it as many times as necessary to make it part of his or her permanent vocabulary. With this approach, it is a good idea to insist the learner use the word in writing and speaking as soon as possible after learning it, in order to make it a truly lasting possession. So, when absorbing a word through this manner, use it over and over again to ensure permanency.

Now, we have hundreds of thousands of words in the English language. It is sometimes frustrating to memorize words one at a time, especially when the pronunciation has little to do with spelling. Here is where the phonetic method can be helpful and save you— the reader, writer, or speller—an incredible amount of frustration. By learning twenty or thirty basic pronunciation rules, you can apply them to thousands and thousands of words, thereby eliminating the task of having to pronounce each word, one at a time.

The rules and examples for each are all common knowledge to elementary school teachers and should have been taught to you between grades one through six. They should then have been reviewed in grades seven through twelve by all of your English teachers to guarantee that they were an integral part of your high school training. But, the truth is, woefully, that very few were taught this material in the first place, and even fewer met up with it anywhere between grades seven and twelve.

Q. "What do those marks above the letters in the dictionary mean?"
A. They are called diacritical marks and they are there to tell you how to pronounce the vowels. Basically, there are two types of vowel sounds: long and short. Every semester, I ask my students the reason

for calling some vowels "long" and some "short," and in twenty-five years of teaching in junior and senior high schools and colleges, not a single student has ever been able to tell me. Do *you* know? I would be pleasantly astonished if you could.

The answer?

As you may know, our sounds are made when the air from our lungs passes over the vocal chords, then up through the throat into the mouth. A number of body parts—throat, mouth, tongue, lips—combine to make the sounds.

If a vowel sound comes out of our mouth and actually says the name of the vowel, we say it is a long vowel sound because it traveled the long distance from the vocal chords out through the lips. Listen: "ate" . . . doesn't the sound of the *a* make the name of the first letter in the alphabet? What about "even?" The first *e* makes the same sound as the name of the fifth letter in the alphabet. "Iron": the *i* says the name of the same letter. "Over": the *o* makes the same sound as the name of that letter. "Cute": the *u* is the same sound as the name of that letter. The lexicographer, the organizer of words in the dictionary, marks the long vowels with a straight line above them. For example, the phonetic spelling of ate is āte. If a vowel does not say its own name, we say it is a short vowel sound. In other words, it travels only a short distance from the vocal chords out through the lips. Examples of phonetically spelled words with short vowel sounds are: băt, lĕt, bĭt, cŏt, cŭt.

Q. "Is the letter Y a vowel or a consonant?"
A. Both! It can be a consonant, as in *yellow* or *canyon*, or a vowel, as in *flying* or *probably*. When there is no other vowel in a word or syllable and there is a *y* present, the *y* becomes the vowel. Y is the only letter in our language that can play either role. (Try to think of it as useful, rather than confusing.)

Study and
Reading Skills

Perhaps I am old-fashioned. Maybe I belong in the dark ages. Why? Because I was brought up on books: fat ones, skinny ones, story books, and ones which introduced me to strangers thousands of miles away. A book, to me, opened doors to lands and adventures which I craved and hungered for the more I read about them. This was no mere spectator sport; it was an opportunity to participate, to march in the parade. It was, and still is, the chance to really be there; the human imagination can be so much more vivid and spectacular than the widest Cinemascope screen. I never fail to wonder at the myriads of adults who stare spellbound at the movie or television screen, mesmerized by adventures so calm, so unmoving, so uninvolving when contrasted with the miraculous imagery capable of being created by this human phenomenon—the imagination.

Why do I read? I use books as a type of therapy, an escape from the here and now into other dimensions, some which soothe, others which excite; all eradicate any pressing worries or concerns. And then I feel refreshed; I am strengthened by my brief sojourn away from this place. I have taken a deep intellectual and emotional breath of fresh invigorating mental oxygen. And I am now ready to face with vigor any irritants and problems which life has to offer.

I receive many questions from the fifty states about reading, perhaps because I am so emotionally involved with books. I am anticipating special interest in this subject on your part. I share this information with you with the fervent desire that you expand and improve your reading skills.

Q. "Are there any simple eye exercises which I can perform to strengthen my ability to read better peripherally and to increase my speed?"
A. Certainly, there are many. Here are a few of the better ones.

Glance briefly at the middle of a license plate. Look away and try to remember all of the letters and numbers. Do the same at a store window. Look very briefly, two seconds perhaps, and then try to recall all of the items in the window. You can repeat this process with other people, too, by simply looking briefly at his or her middle and then recollecting clothing type, color of shoes, and so forth.

Another excellent method for improving your peripheral span is to take a pencil or pen, move it slowly past the right (or left) side of your head at eye level, pass it to the other hand behind your head and bring it slowly around the other side. As you move it to the rear of your head, follow it as far as you can until it disappears from sight; then pick it up on the other side as it reappears. I would attempt this exercise once per day. It works. Move your eyes in short diagonal sweeps down the page starting in the upper left hand corner and ending in the bottom right corner. Try this on page 85.

Q. "A young man preparing for final exams in high school called and asked, 'I have so much material to study. How can I pick out the main ideas?' "
A. Here are a few hints. Most important, the more practice you get, the better you will become. Finding the main idea requires a lot of repetition. It is not an easy skill to acquire, but it can be done! Remember that each paragraph is a separate thought unit, possessing one sentence, usually the first or the last, which expresses the main idea of the paragraph. This is the topic sentence.

Most writers tend to emphasize main ideas by repeating them. If you find an idea restated, it is probably an important one.

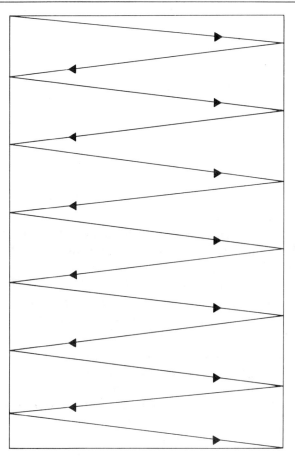

You can find topic sentences in four different locations within the paragraph:

1. At the beginning
2. At the end
3. In the middle
4. One at the start, another at the end.

Some authors will place very important material in *italics*. Others will give summaries at the end of chapters which highlight the main

ideas. Others will place questions about important points at the end
of a chapter. If you have a good author, the questions will be in the
same order as the material in the chapter, and the questions are really
an excellent outline of the most important points in the chapter.
Finally, important or main ideas may be printed in heavy letters which
stand out from the rest of the page.

Q. "Why is reading important, and what is a powerful reader?"
A. Through books and the beautiful words they contain, we have a
link from the present to the past and future. When we read, our
minds join with the great minds of all ages. Author and reader can
communicate from country to country, dimension to dimension, century to century. Reading is the best method we have of learning from
the accomplishments and mistakes of others, to build on the former
and learn.

A powerful reader is one who can sound out all the letters and
letter combinations in words, and build a stock of words—a mountain
of words, if possible—and then combine these words into groups,
combinations, which evolve into ideas. Some reading involves the
identification of specific words (facts, dates, names) but most reading
involves the assimilation of word groups, *ideas*, into the brain to be
digested and then built upon. This process, where the human brain
can receive ideas and then produce new ones of its own, we do not
fully comprehend. But we are all capable of doing it, and it is a miracle
for which we should be thankful.

Q. "What are the worst reading habits, and how do I overcome them
by myself ?"
A. Where shall I begin? There are so many negative reading habits
which interfere with the normal process of good reading. Most of us
have been practicing these poor habits, or at least some of them, for
as long as we have been reading. I'll start with the most common and
show you how to remedy the situation by yourself. If these habits are
overcome—and they can be with practice—your reading speed, concentration, and comprehension will all improve markedly.

Many readers still unconsciously say the words to themselves, using their vocal chords as they read. Are you doing this? It's called sub-vocalizing. As you read to yourself, gently touch or palpate your throat with the tips of your fingers. If you feel a vibration, then you are probably saying the words to yourself. To stop, put your tongue to the roof of your mouth. You may still be able to make noises, but they will be unrecognizable as words to you or anyone. Soon, you will cease making these latter noises, and the habit will be broken.

The other type of sub-vocalization is mental. When you read, do you either see or hear the individual words in your imagination? If you do, it is not uncommon, but it does indicate that you are reading word by word, not phrase by phrase. When you expand your peripheral span, that is, read three or four words with each fixation or stop of your eyes, you will then be sending to the brain not individual words but the ideas formed by the groupings of these words. At that point, you will no longer see or hear the words in your brain. So, to decrease mental subvocalization, increase peripheral span.

Another common bad reading habit is the moving of the head or neck as you read. You should be reading with your eyes, and your eyes only, not your head or neck, should be moving from left to right and from top of page down to the bottom. If you are aware of this unnecessary movement, simply grasp your head or neck in your hands and hold it still as you read. If you have been moving your head while you read for many years, it probably means that your eyes have been moving very little during the act of reading. So, once the head moving has stopped, your eyes will probably feel some strain as they move across the page. This is very much like doing pushups for the first time in your life. The eye muscles aren't used to this type of exercise. Gently place the palms of your hands over your eyes, don't push or rub, and let the warmth from your palms soothe the eye muscles. Each time your eyes feel tired from reading, relax them with your hands for a few seconds. That's all it takes.

When reading to themselves many readers move their lips as if they were reading out loud. This is called verbalization. It slows down their reading. To correct verbalization or lip reading place your fist between your lips. It works.

If you have more than one bad reading habit, don't worry. Concentrate on overcoming one habit at a time.

Do you find yourself losing the place on the page? Many people use a finger or a pencil down the side of the page to keep track of where they are. This takes away your eyes' responsibility to move from one line to the next. The movement from one line to the next should be like a rolling ocean wave, smooth and gentle. If you practice following the arrows in the exercise on page 85 for a minute or two each day, your eyes will soon become accustomed to the same movements on a page of print. Then you will no longer skip lines or lose your place.

Another very bad and common reading habit is what we call regressing. Have you ever read a page and almost unconsciously found yourself going back over what you had already read? Perhaps it was a textbook or technological work from which you had to glean important information. As you read each paragraph, you had a terrifying feeling that you had forgotten the most important facts in the preceding paragraphs, so you allowed your eyes to glance back up the page. Most probably, by the time you finished reading a page, you had reread most of it, in bits and snatches, three or four times. Obviously, you would be reading much more quickly if the page were perused only once, with maximum retention of information.

How do you get to the bottom of the page without going back over the information several times? There are two solutions to this problem. The first is to simply cover the page with another piece of paper: and, as you read the page, just move the other paper down, covering what you have already read. Obviously, if it is covered you cannot read it again.

But, I like another remedy far better. Remember, in a race, you cannot ask the referee to rerun the race, to give you a second chance. You get one chance and only one chance, and if you don't win, you lose. And this rule applies to everything you read. There is simply too much in one lifetime to digest. You cannot possibly read all the books that are on the shelves of the library. So, when you choose or are assigned a book to read, run your race and win, read the book well and swiftly, for there are many other books to read, and if you take too much time with one volume, you will never receive the opportunity to get to others. So, a faster reader and a reader with no bad reading habits is a power reader.

Q. "With my job, getting home late, tired, the television seems to be the easiest way to be entertained. I have never been able to become involved totally in a book. Is there an easy way to cross over that magic line between spectator and participant?"

A. Now that is a vital question. And I have what I consider to be a great answer. I know it is a fine solution because so many of my clients have told me so. Here it is: Can anyone teach you to fall in love? Of course it's impossible. But it is possible to show you how to become involved with the characters and situations in books. I grew up in the age of radio. My imagination could run wild as I cowered under the sheets listening to squeaking doors and mysterious sounds emanating from the airwaves. For many years now, all we have had for home entertainment is television. It does all the work for us. All we have to do is sit and watch.

Lately, however, there has been a resurgence of radio drama. I ask all of my students and private clients to listen to at least one hour per week of drama on the radio. Guess what? Their imaginations come alive and, as a direct result, with little effort on their part, they are able to enter the pages of the books they are reading, almost merge with the characters, live their lives and experiences. For them, books have become a rich, full, magnificent experience. As a matter of fact, many have told me that not a day goes by without their spending two or three hours curled up with their favorite author living through his tales as if they were their very own. This is bibliomania, a madness I have enjoyed for forty-seven years. I hope fervently that it becomes yours also.

There seems to be a direct relationship between the awakening of the imagination through listening to radio, and the application of that newly discovered imagination to the reading of books. Anything that works for others is worth trying for yourself. Try it; you'll like it!

Another suggestion I have for involvement in books is to read a short story, stop before finishing it, then write the ending yourself. You'll get to know the characters as if they were personal friends. The process is called "closure."

I must add this to end my answer. Many books, short stories and poetry in particular, can be read aloud with others as listeners. The

sounding of the words brings many of them alive, and it's so good to
shut the eyes and be lulled into the world of dreams and imaginings
by the sound of beautiful phrases and descriptive passages that evoke
in one's mind scenes of love, of battles fought and won, of heroic
acts, and events which bring tears to the eyes and cause laughter to
bubble from the soul.

Q. "Is there such a thing as speed reading, and is it worthwhile?"
A. Is there a God? Are vitamins worthwhile? Are the Republicans
better or worse than the Democrats? Any answer you receive to these
really unanswerable queries can only reflect the opinion of the speaker
or writer. I promise not to deliver any sermons on this or any other
topic about which I am asked, but I will offer a personal opinion based
on observations, personal experience, and the reading of countless
books and treatises on the subject. I feel very strongly about this
topic, but it is certainly open to argument, even though I know, as
one of the world's leading experts on the teaching of literacy, that
my feelings are correct.

First, let me define speed as I perceive it. It is the reading rate
at which we can sound out words, define them, and combine them
into ideas quickly. Therefore, depending upon the task at hand, speed
varies according to the reading assignment and the amount of time
available to achieve that assignment.

How do you determine your reading speed? A simple obvious
formula will suffice. Count the number of words in a given line of
print, multiply it by the number of lines read on a page, and divide
by the number of minutes spent reading that amount of matter. If
you become impatient when you read, your mind wanders, you probably are reading too slowly. It should be mentioned that mind wandering and impatience could be symptoms of other situations: personal
or emotional problems, poor diet, faulty vision. Obviously, to be a
powerful reader, you cannot allow external stimuli to interfere with
the reading act; your diet, as discussed in a different chapter, should
be excellent, and you should have your eyes examined by a qualified
ophthalmologist or optometrist.

You were probably taught in elementary school that reading de-
mands the identification of every word on a page. This point was
doubly emphasized because, you must remember, you were called

upon almost every day to read out loud. How well I remember those mortifying times when I couldn't identify a specific word. There was total silence in the classroom as I struggled to recognize that vicious animal on that page that was causing me extreme mortification and embarrassment. Oh, the silence as my friends endeavored to help by subtly whispering what they thought the word was across the classroom, and my enemies gleefully snickered into their readers, relishing my discomfort.

The point here is that it was impressed upon us early in our educational careers that a good reader read every word. And, to this very day, some types of reading require word-by-word reading: technical books, text books, often, some best sellers. Minimum speed could mean one word each minute or two. Maximum speed? Quite often, it is necessary to be able to read ideas, not individual words. The author expressed herself and her ideas in groups or clumps of words. If I wish to express my feelings for you, I say, "I love you," not "I   love   you." The sentiment is composed of the three words said as a unified group or whole; they are almost tied to each other. Therefore, to be understood, they should be read as a group.

If you are now reading

one   word   at   a   time,

practice reading

two words   each time   that you   read sentences.

To do this, take a pencil and place a dot between and just above every two words in a newspaper, like this.

·   ·   ·   ·

The situation   in Europe   is getting   to be
really more   than we   can understand.

If you look at the dots, moving your eyes as rapidly and comfortably as you can from dot to dot, you have now doubled your reading speed. Once you have mastered this technique, place your dots in the middle and just above every three words; when you've mastered that, every four. When you are able to comprehend the general meaning of every three or four words with minimal effort, and good understanding, you have not only tripled or quadrupled your reading speed, you are now what I call a fast reader. But, remember a fast reader is not necessarily a good reader. There will always be times when you must slow down. But for heaven's sake, don't have guilt feelings about reading very, very slowly (or very, very quickly).

Q. "Are there are different kinds of reading?"

A. The various types of reading are:

1. *Skimming.* This is the most rapid of all reading rates, and the most complex. On the basis of the most recent results of eye movement photography, it is safe to say that anyone who claims to be reading faster than 800 to 900 words per minute is skimming.

   That is, the reader is not reading every word, sentence, or even every paragraph, but is skipping with judgment. Thus, for most human beings, those who claim rates of one-to-two-thousand words per minute are approaching the realms of quackery, if they also claim to be quality readers. But skimming is a necessary skill to learn, especially when reviewing a textbook.

2. *Fast Reading.* This is the quickest rate at which virtually every word can be read. This is usually accomplished, at first, by using devices designed to improve reading speed, then gradually teaching readers to be able to do this by themselves usually when they have developed their peripheral span to take in three or four words at a glance.

3. *Deep Reading.* This is used for material that requires slow, careful reading and even rereading. Textbooks, contracts, mechanical specifications, love letters require that every word, phrase, every punctuation mark is noted. This is careful, critical reading.

4. *Reading for Pleasure.* This is the rate for personal or recreational reading. There is no determined striving for any special rate or time limit. The main goal is pleasure; a secondary goal may be the obtaining of information. Recreational reading speeds can vary: the reader may skim through a long descriptive passage; an action packed scene, full of blood and thunder, may be read rapidly. Special sections or key paragraphs that provide vital information may call for intensive reading. However, the main objective is personal pleasure.

Etymology: The History
of Specific Words

In many ways, words are like people. They are born, grow up, have offspring, grow old, retire, and die. Over the course of the years, words change their meanings; what they originally meant is often quite different from their meaning today. At one time, the word *nice* was not such a nice word at all. Its original meaning was "silly" (from Latin *nescius*, "ignorant"). "Cohort" originally meant one-tenth of a Roman legion. Today, it means an associate or companion. Companion literally meant someone with whom you broke bread— *com*, "with" and *pain*, "bread." It's easy to see that someone with whom one ate regularly might become a companion. The same with *comrade*, whose original meaning was someone with whom one shared a room. The words *chili* and *pickle* had an offspring—it is piccalilli, thought to be a combination of the two. *Rumbullion* grew old, retired and died, but its offspring—rum—survives. Some of the callers to the National Grammar Hotline show an intense interest in the origins of words. We have selected some of the most interesting to include in this chapter.

Q. "Is *abracadabra* really a mystical incantation?"
A. Yes! It is a word held to possess supernatural powers to ward off disease or disaster, and it derives from the Late Greek *abrasadabra*,

a magic word used by a Gnostic sect, probably derived from *Abrasax*, the name of a Gnostic deity.

Q. *"Absurd* is a funny word. What do you know about it?"
A. *Ab* is a prefix meaning "away from" and *surd*, derives from Latin *surdus*, "deaf." In Latin, the word *absurdus* means "away from the right sound." Today, someone or something which is "absurd" is foolish, unreasonable. But, to the Romans, it was something or someone "turning a deaf ear to the right sound."

Q. "I am the public relations director of my company, and we're always acquiring new companies. Which is the better word to use for these acquisitions, *affiliates* or *subsidiaries?"*
A. Affiliate is Latin—*affiliatus*, past participle of *affiliare* "to adopt as a son." So an affiliate is actually an "adopted son." Subsidiary comes from Latin *subsidere*, the literal meaning of which is "to sit down and remain." So between the two, "affiliate" would seem to have the more appropriate meaning.

Q. "My grandmother says those little white doilies that people used to put on the backs and arms of chairs are named after a hair oil. She calls them *antimacassars.* Is she right?"
A. Yes, she is. *Anti-* of course is the Greek prefix for against; the little white doily was there to protect the chairs from macassar oil, which men of the late nineteenth century once applied to their hair.

Q. "Why do we call spiders *arachnids?"*
A. They are named after Arachne, a maiden in Greek mythology who was transformed into a spider by the goddess Athena for daring to challenge her to a weaving contest.

Q. "Does the word *assassin* have anything to do with hashish?"
A. Yes. During the time of the Crusades, a secret Moslem society terrorized their enemies by performing murders as a religious duty, often under the influence of hashish. These killers became known as *hasheeshin* ("eaters or smokers of hashish"). Eventually, the word assassin in English came to mean any murderer.

Q. "Where does our word for book of maps—*atlas*—come from?"
A. If you remember your Greek myths, Atlas was a giant, condemned to support the heavens on his shoulders for all time. Early books of maps frequently included a picture of Atlas carrying the world.

Q. "Why do we call a vote a *ballot*?"
A. Because a small ball or pebble (Italian *ballotta*) was originally used for voting. In ancient Athens, jurors used one color of ball for acquittal and a different color—usually black—for condemnation. Even today, some clubs accept or reject members on the basis of a vote taken with a white or black ball, from whence comes our word *blackball*— "to vote against, or to reject." Incidentally, *bullet* has no relationship to ballot, although one would suspect it did. Bullet is a descendant of the Latin *bulla*—"bubble", then through French, *boulette*, where it meant "little ball."

Q. "Are *bizarre* and *bazaar* related? I have this idea that because odd and unusual, bizarre things, might be found at a bazaar, that perhaps they are."
A. Sorry to disappoint you! Bizarre comes from the French *bizarre* meaning "odd." But this has drifted far afield from its original meaning, which was handsome, brave. It is thought to derive from a Basque word *bizar*, meaning "beard." (Bearded hence spirited.) We can only guess what bizarre things happened to change bizarre from "bearded and handsome" to "odd."

Bazaar is an Oriental market, from the Persian word *bazar*, (Middle Persian *bachar*, Old Persian *abecharish*).

Q. "My son was given this spelling word by his fourth grade teacher, *brobdingnagian*. Is it real?"
A. Remember *Gulliver's Travels* by Jonathan Swift? Two countries visited by him were Lilliput, where the people were tiny, and Brobdingnag, the land of giants. Thanks to Swift, we have *brobdingnagian*, meaning "huge" and *lilliputian*, meaning "tiny."

Q. "Doesn't our word *chauffeur* come from the French word chauffer, meaning 'to heat?' How did it come to mean what it does today?"

A. You're absolutely correct. The original chauffeurs drove steam-powered automobiles, and their first task was to heat up the engine until a sufficient head of steam had built up to propel the car. So the chauffeur, if you were lucky enough to have one, was someone who heated up, steamed up the auto so it could run.

Q. "What is a *clerihew?*"
A. It's a four-line humorous verse about a person whose name is given in the first line, invented by E. Clerihew Bentley. Two famous clerihews:

> Sir Christopher Wren
> Said "I'm going to dine with some men
> If anyone calls
> Say I'm designing St. Paul's."

> It was weakness of Voltaire's
> To forget to say his prayers
> And one which, to his shame
> He never overcame.

Q. "Why do we pronounce *colonel* 'kernel'?"
A. The answer goes back to the sixteenth century when it was spelled coronel. The word was pronounced as spelled, at first, and later elided to "kernel." Colonel is a French word which comes from the Old Italian *colonello* (commander of a column of soldiers, and before that from the Latin *columna*.) Samuel Johnson, who wrote the first dictionary, often insisted on keeping the original Latin spelling, and it may be (although it's not known) that Johnson retained or reinstituted the *l* in colonel.

Q. "I suspect there's a good story behind *cuckold.*"
A. As you know, it is a name given to a man whose wife has committed adultery. The origin is thought to be the Old French *cucu*, "cuckoo," perhaps because cuckoos leave their eggs in the nests of other birds.

Q. "Why is the name of the thing I'm always on—a *diet*—also used for a legislature, or assembly? I suspect there's a story there."

A. You suspect correctly. Diet's original meaning—"habitually taken food and drink"—derives from the Greek *diaita,* from the verb *diaitan,* which means "to lead one's life" or "to govern." In the Greek, *diaita* was used for a way of life prescribed by a physician, a diet or other regimen.

The other diet is a derivative of the Latin word *dies,* "day." Medieval Latin *dieta* was used for "a day's journey, a day's work," or "a day's wages" and also for "a particular day set for a meeting or assembly." Later diet came to be the term for the assembly itself. Today Japan calls its general legislative assembly the Diet, and the semiannual general assembly of the estates of the Holy Roman Empire was known as the Diet.

Q. "Where does the word *dingbat* (Archie's favorite name for Edith in 'All in the Family') come from?"
A. It's a great synonym for "peculiar" or "odd," and it derives from printing. Printers use the word dingbat to describe a variety of typographical ornaments not easy to describe precisely. (In Australia, "the dingbats" is an acute hangover.)

Q. "I just graduated and received my *diploma.* Was this originally a Greek word?"
A. Yes; diploma comes from the Greek word *diploos,* meaning "something folded twice." Originally a diploma was a piece of parchment folded twice.

Q. "Where do we get that good old crossword puzzle word *eleemosynary?*"
A. It's a fascinating word with a direct derivation from the Medieval Latin *eleemosynarius,* from Late Latin *eleemosyna,* alms. I didn't know this word until my questioner asked about it. It means "charitable."

Q. "How did *extra,* Latin for 'outside' and *vagant,* which is Latin for 'wandering' come to be linked in *extravagant* and ultimately mean 'given to lavish or imprudent expenditure'?"

A. I see you have been exposed to some Latin. Extravagant does, indeed, mean "wandering about," in its literal sense. Thus an "extravagant" person was one who "travelled beyond the limits of his immediate environs." Gradually, the word came to describe someone or something who exceeded good limits—wandered or strayed too far from moderation and balance. Eventually, it came to mean "spending much more than necessary." This is another good illustration of the way words drift, through the years, away from their original meaning.

Q. *"Folly?* A direct reduction of foolishness?"
A. Yes. Folly is the condition or quality of being foolish; it comes to us from Middle English *folie,* from Old French *fol,* "foolish," from Latin *follis,* "bellows" or "windbag."

Q. "How did the word *fornication* come to mean sexual intercourse? Doesn't the Latin root of the word mean 'vault' or 'arch'? That's what my dictionary says."
A. Your dictionary is right and, if you'll notice, it also lists "arched or vaulted" as an alternate meaning for "fornicate." But here's the story. Because brothels were frequently housed in the Roman vaults, the word came to be first a synonym for brothel, and then a synonym for what took place in brothels, or sexual intercourse. The word is derived from the Latin *fornix,* meaning "vault, arched basement."

Q. "What do *gauche* and *Gaucho* have in common?"
A. Absolutely nothing! Gauche, which means "awkward of manner, clumsy," comes from the French word *gauche,* meaning "left" (as opposed to "right"). How the word's meaning evolved from left to awkward, we can only surmise. Gaucho, on the other hand, is a cowboy of the South American pampas. He derives his name (most likely) from the Quechuan word *wahcha,* meaning "a poor person, a vagabond." The words are pronounced differently: gowsh and gowcho.

Q. "What is the origin of the word *glamor?*"
A. Believe it or not, as Robert Ripley used to say, it is *grammar!* During the middle ages, learning came to be associated with a kind

of magic, as it was couched in a language not understood by ordinary folk. Magic, as well as astrology, was part of *grammatica*. Scholars were viewed with awe by ordinary folk. In Scotland, the connection between grammar and magic produced the word *glamer* (or glamour, as the British spell it). As the word evolved, it came into its present day meaning: compelling (almost supernatural) charm.

Q. "I would hazard a guess that the word *hazard* has an interesting derivation. It sounds Persian."
A. You're close. It actually comes from an Arabic word—*az-zahr*—meaning "a die, one of a pair of dice." Hazard was a game invented, according to the twelfth-century French archbishop and historian William of Tyre, to pass the time during the siege of a castle in Palestine. The word became "hazard" in Medieval English, and what was once a risk based upon the roll of the dice soon became a risk of any kind.

Q. "I know that hors d'oeuvre's literal meaning is 'outside the work' but where does *canape* come from? I often serve both."
A. It has a fascinating derivation. As we know it, a canape is a thin piece of bread or toast spread with cheese, meat, or relish and served as an appetizer. The word comes from a French word meaning "couch," which makes sense if you think of it as a seat for the relish; it has an actual cousinship to the word *canopy*. Canopy comes, via the Middle English *canape* or *canope*, from the Medieval Latin *canapeum* (a couch with a mosquito net) which may have originated in the Greek city of Kanopos and was probably influenced by the Greek word for mosquito, *konops*. Today "canape" refers to the seat for the appetizer, and "canopy" refers to the cloth covering which presumably keeps the konops, or mosquitos, away.

Q. "Can you break down *iconoclastic* or *iconoclast* for me?"
A. Sure, It literally means an icon breaker, one who breaks established ideas and images, and it comes from Medieval Latin *icono* (= image) and *clastes* (= breaker). It was applied to opponents of the use and veneration of icons in the Eastern Churches during the

eighth and ninth centuries. Today, it means anyone who seeks to overthrow traditional ideas or institutions.

Q. "Does *intoxicate* have something to do with *toxic*, which is poison?"

A. Yes it does. Intoxicate, besides meaning "to get drunk," also means "to stimulate or excite," but the root word is Latin—*toxicum*, meaning poison. Think about that the next time you have too much to drink. Incidentally, Benjamin Franklin once drew up a list of 228 euphemisms current in his day for drunkenness, beginning with "intoxication." How many can you think of? Writing in *A Dictionary of American Slang*, Harold Wentworth and Stuart Berg Flexner note that the concept having the most slang synonyms is "drunk." Furthermore, few of these synonyms are derogatory or critical. Many of the words are quite old.

Q. "Did someone named Leo invent or design *leotards*?"

A. Jules Léotard, a nineteenth century trapeze artist, designed the close fitting costume so he could more readily perform his aerial somersault, he being the first to do so, in the Circus Napoleon in Paris. Here are some other people who gave their name to things:

begonia	During the reign of Louis XIII, Michel Bégon brought the plant to France from Santo Domingo, where he had served as governor.
bloomer	Amelia Jenks Bloomer, nineteenth-century women's liberationist and temperance society leader, was the first to wear "her skirts all the way up to her knees and the lower half of her legs encased in a kind of Turkish trouser."
bowdlerize	Thomas Bowdler gave the world an edition of Shakespeare's works with the naughty or otherwise improper bits tactfully left out.
hansom	Joseph Aloysius Hansom registered his design for the "safety cab" in 1834. Hansom cabs soon became the most popular in London.
mackintosh	Charles MacIntosh discovered fabric could be waterproofed by cementing two thicknesses of cloth together with India rubber.

magnolia	Named after Pierre Magnol, who was a contemporary of Michel Bégon during the reign of Louis XIII.
martinet	General Jean Martinet instituted strict discipline into the French infantry (and introduced the use of the bayonet in battle) during the mid-seventeenth century.

There are many others. If this subject is of particular interest to you, your library can guide you to books which deal with this subject.

Q. "I've always wondered why the word *love* is used to designate "no score" in a tennis match. It seems like an odd term to use in sports. What's the story?"

A. An egg-shaped zero marks the "love" score—which is no score—and the French words for "the egg" are *l'oeuf.* Tennis came to England from France. The English found *l'oeuf* troublesome, so the term was modified into a word they know—love.

Q. "What can you tell me about *map?*"

A. *Mappa* is the Latin word for "cloth"; early maps were drawn on cloth. By the late Latin period, *mappa* had changed to *nappa.* This went into Old French as *nappe,* meaning cloth, and even today, *nappe* in French means "tablecloth." *Nappe* is also the derivation of our words napkin and napery (and also apron, because the word was originally napron: "a napron" soon became "an apron" with the *n* sliding off to the left).

Maps, of course, are flat. This led to another term for map—*plat,* from the Greek *platy,* Latin *plata* meaning "flat." We still use *plat,* in its variant form *plot,* today.

Q. "I love a *mystery,* and I love the word. It's so euphonious. What do you know about its origin?"

A. It comes from a Greek word *mystes* meaning "close-mouthed." There were many secret religious societies in Greece, and anyone who was initiated into these societies had to be "close-mouthed" and never reveal the secret rites. The word "mystery" gradually came to mean anything that was secret or hidden.

Q. "My name is James, but my *nickname* is Jim. Did someone take a knife and "nick" a piece out of James to come up with Jim?"
A. No. A nickname is an additional name given to someone or something to help identify him or it. The original Middle English word expressed this idea clearly. *Eke* meant "an addition or extension." It was combined with the word "name," making an *ekename:* an additional name. The word ekename evolved to nekename and, in modern spelling, became nickname.

Q. "What does a *nightmare* have to do with horses?"
A. Absolutely nothing. The *mare* of nightmare comes from another word *mare*, found in Old English, which meant "an evil spirit thought to oppress people during sleep." The word nightmare first appeared in Middle English in the thirteenth century. In the sixteenth century, the word was extended to unpleasant dreams, no doubt from the belief that such dreams were caused by the sinister mare—the evil spirit.

Q. "I know the Pacific Ocean is called "pacific" after the Spanish word for "peace." What does the *Atlantic* Ocean mean, and how was it named?"
A. It derives from Greek myths, according to Isaac Asimov's *Words From the Myths*. The Atlantides were Greek nymphs associated with the sea. Other such nymphs were the Oceanids, the daughters of Oceanus, and the Nereids, the daughters of an old god of the sea named Nereus. The Atlantides were associated with the far western waters, so those waters were called "Atlantic"; today, we call it the "Atlantic Ocean." Whenever I fly over the Atlantic, I say to my wife, "Doesn't that look pacific down there?"

Q. "Where does our word *pay* come from?"
A. It comes from the Latin *pacare*, meaning "to make peaceful." It is a good illustration of how words change and refine their meaning down through the years. One can assume that years ago, when a man or woman got his/her "pay," he/she became peaceful. One can observe the same phenomenon today.

Q. "I would guess that the word *peddler* must be one of the oldest in our language. What's its origin?"

A. One who travelled about selling wares for a living often carried his wares in a *pedde,* Middle English for "a covered basket," and that's how he got his name.

Q. "Straighten me out on the word *playwright.* Why isn't it spelled playwrite, because, after all, that's what it means—someone who writes plays."

A. It's not spelled play*write* because the *wright* on the end means "a person who constructs something." So the word means someone who constructs plays. There are also *shipwrights,* carpenters employed in the construction or maintenance of ships, *wheelwrights,* and others.

Q. "What's a *portmanteau word?*"

A. Actually it's one that is "packed together" as in a portmanteau, or suitcase. Lewis Carroll, creator of *Alice in Wonderland* and *Through the Looking Glass,* was a great exponent of the portmanteau word, creating jabberwocky by blending two words into one: *slithy* (lithe and slimy) as well as *mimsy,* which was created from "miserable" and "flimsy." Carroll himself described these as "portmanteau" words, because they were packed together. *Smog* is also a portmanteau word, a combination of fog and smoke. I'm sure you can think of many more, such as: smaze—smoke and haze, sunder—sun and thunder, or sneet—snow and sleet.

Q. "*Queue*—I thought that this was a stick used for playing pool."

A. You have the correct pronunciation but not the right meaning or spelling. In pool, it is spelled cue. A queue has its origin in a Latin word meaning "tail." In present English—more in England than in America, although it is gaining in popularity here—it means a line, preferably a straight one, like a tail. Both words have the same pronunciations.

Q. "And what's the derivation of *quixotic?*"

A. It comes directly from Don Quixote, who you may remember was caught up in the romance of noble deeds, romantic without regard to practicality. He loved to tilt at windmills. So, too, do many of us love to joust with improbabilities.

Q. "What do *river* and *rival* have in common?"
A. Rival is derived from the Latin *rivalis,* an adjective which means "of a brook or stream," (from *rivus,* "brook or stream"). As a noun, *rivalis* refers to those who use the same stream as a source of water. Since quarrels over water rights are legendary, those who came to use the same water sources came into English as "rivals." The Old French *rivere* or *riviere* is the direct source for our word "river."

Q. "I know what a *chasm* is, but what's a *sar?* And do *sarcasm* and chasm have an affinity?"
A. A sar is flesh and it comes from the Greek *sarx,* meaning flesh. The suffix, *casm,* means "to cut." Derivation of the word: *sarkazein,* a Greek verb meaning "to tear flesh like dogs." The Greek noun *sarkasmos* means essentially the same thing as it does in English today: a biting or cutting remark.

As for chasm, its root the Greek *khasma* via the Latin *chasma.* Both mean "to yawn, to gape," or "a yawning gulf."

Q. "What is the derivation of the word *school?*"
A. How words and their meanings change! Its original meaning was "leisure." The Greek *skhole* means leasure, as does the Latin word *schola.* We can guess at the connection. Since the Greeks felt that if one had "leisure," one would naturally desire to spend it in studying and learning, the connection made sense in their society. *Skhole* became Old English *scol.* (St. Augustine of Canterbury is said to have established the first English school in 598.) *Scol* evolved into *scole* in Middle English and then into school. The Phi Delta Kappa magazine, incidentally, noted that books, used in school, actually mean Built On Organized Knowledge, a marvelous acronym, but just a spoof?

Q. "What can you tell me about the word which describes my occupation, *secretary.* Wasn't its original meaning 'a desk'?"
A. No, actually the word goes back to the Middle Ages and comes from the Latin *secretus,* "secret." A "*secretarius*" was a confidential

officer, one who could be trusted with secrets of state. Later, the
word was also applied to the desk at which the secretary worked.
From the same Latin word, we also get:

secretariat	the department administered by a government secretary
secrete	to conceal in a hiding place
secretion	the process of secreting a substance
secretive	close-mouthed
secretary	performing the function of secretion
secret service	intelligence work by a government agency

Q "I've often wondered why letters are signed '*Sincerely.*' "
A. The word means literally "without wax": from the Latin *sine,*
"without" and *cera,* "wax." There are two theories why something
"without wax" was deemed good, or truthful. One is that chipped
pottery was often covered with wax to make it appear whole, and
sold as though in perfect condition, so pottery "sine cera" was more
trustworthy. Another theory has to do with the purest grade of honey,
cleaned of the wax which might be left over from the honeycomb.

Q. "What is the derivation of the word *slave?*"
A. In the Middle Ages, the Germanic and Slavic peoples fought one
another. Conquered Slavs were bought and sold in western Europe.
The Latin word *Sclavus,* "Slav," came to mean "slave" as well. By the
tenth century, the word was used to designate any human chattel, of
whatever ethnic origin.

Q. "*Spelunker* is an odd word for someone who explores caves. Where
does it come from?"
A. It can be traced back more than two thousand years to the Latin
word for "cave," *spelunca.*

Q. "My mother transposes syllables, sometimes quite amusingly. The
other day she said, 'Here comes Mr. Clown with his brass' instead
of 'Here comes Mr. Brown with his class.' There's a word for this,
isn't there?"

A. Yes, it's *spoonerism*, named after the Reverend William A. Spooner, Dean and later Warden of New College, Oxford. Spooner was an albino with very poor eyesight and a nervous tendency to transpose syllables while speaking, a habit which endeared him to his students.

Two famous spoonerisms: in chapel, one day, he announced the next hymn as "Kinquering Congs . . ." and he once reprimanded one of his students by telling him, "You have deliberately tasted two worms, and you must leave Oxford by the town drain."

Q. "Why do we call a potato a *spud*?"

A. A spud was, and is, a sharp spade used to dig up potatoes.

Q. "I suspect *supercilious* has an interesting derivation."

A. You suspect correctly. *Cilium*, singular, *cilia*, plural, means "eye lash(es)." Supercilious means "scornful, disdainful," and people who are supercilious often have the habit of raising their eyelids and/or eyebrows over some disdained situation. It appears, by raising the brows, that one is looking down at others. Don't you agree?

Q. "Where do our words *television* and *video* come from?"

A. *Tele* is a Greek prefix meaning "at a distance" or "far off." *Vision* need no explanation. *Video* is Latin for "I see." TV, incidentally, is an acronym, not an abbreviation, and requires no periods after the T and the V.

Q. "The word 'tie' sounds very British but its synonym, *cravat*, sounds foreign. Is it?"

A. You have a good ear. The word originally referred to a native of Croatia, the Croats, known in French as *cravats*. The original cravats were scarves worn around the necks of Croatian soldiers. Around 1637, the French army formed a regiment of light cavalry, dressed in imitation of the Croatian uniforms, including the elegant neck scarf. The fashion was adopted by the men of Paris, and men have been wearing neckties or cravats ever since. The word "necktie," incidentally, simply describes a cravat.

Q. "How did a funny word like '*tip*' come to mean a sum of money left in return for good service?"

A. There are several theories. A popular one is that it was coined from the first letters of signs TO INSURE PROMPTNESS which were posted on coin boxes on coffee house tables of Dr. Johnson's day. The other is that it is a corruption of the word "stipend."

Q. "Do the words *tryst* and *triste* have an affiliation or common root?"
A. No. Tryst, a secret meeting between young lovers, derives from Old French *triste,* an appointed station in hunting. We can only surmise that the old hunting lodge, deserted between hunts, was an excellent place for a tryst. Your word *triste,* which is Spanish and also French, comes from a different root (even though it's spelled the same way): the Latin *tristis,* meaning "gloomy."

Q. "Can you tell me the origin of the word *trivia?* I'm a trivia fan."
A. The word, as you know, means "unimportant" or "of little consequence." Its origin lies in "three roads" which came together in ancient Rome. *Tri* means ' three" in Latin—*via* means "roads." At the conjunction of these roads people would gather and exchange small talk—sort of like our present-day office water cooler, where people often gather to discuss "trivia."

Q. "I play the *ukulele.* What is the origin of the word?"
A. It literally means "jumping flea": *uku* being Hawaiian for "flea" and *lele* meaning "jumping." King Kalakaua, it is said, gave the instrument its name. Instead of describing the instrument, he was actually describing a man, one Edward Purvis, a former British army officer living in Hawaii and an official at the court, who was short and lively. When Purvis learned to play a small stringed instrument which Portuguese immigrants brought to the island, *his* nickname, ukulele, was given to the instrument as well. Wouldn't you like an instrument named after you?

Q. "*Ululate.* I always remember it by thinking 'her father howled when I brought Lulu home late.' This word sounds like a howl. What do you know about it?"
A. I like your way of connecting howl with ululate. And some in-

teresting old words are also connected with it: the German *uwwalon*, "owl"; Old English *ule*, "owl"; Middle Dutch *hulen*, "to howl" (like an owl). The Latin word *ululare*, "to howl" is the direct source of the word in English.

Q. "I like the word *wry*, and people often say I have a wry sense of humor. What can you tell me about wry?"
A. A person with a wry sense of humor is said to be "dryly humorous, often with a touch of irony." The word comes from Middle English *wrien*, which means "to bend, twist, turn aside." So, if you like, a wry sense of humor could literally be a twisted sense of humor!

Q. "I often have a *yen* for more linguistic knowledge. For example, I want to know what 'yen' means."
A. You're literally exhibiting a "craving for opium" because that is what the word means. Chinese immigrating to the United States in the 1880s brought the word *in-yan* with them. It later became *yen yen*. Eventually, the duplication was abandoned, and the word became *yen*. In 1886, a policeman wrote of the opium addiction common in the city thusly: "A friend suffering with the *inyun* is a man to be avoided."

Curiosities

Q. "What's the derivation of *A-1*, meaning 'best?' "
A. It was originally used by Lloyds Register in London in describing its rating of ships and its estimate of a ship's insurance risk. Its derivation is, of course, from the first letter of the alphabet and the first number.

Q. "I know that B.C. after a date, such as '44 B.C.,' stands for 'before Christ.' What does A.D. stand for, as in 1898 A.D.?"
A. It stands for *Anno Domini* which is Latin for "in the year of our Lord." Incidentally, B.C. always goes after the date and A.D. before. So your example should read A.D. 1898.

Q. "*Adios*, of course, is Spanish for 'goodbye,' and its literal meaning is 'go with God.' What about *adieu?*"
A. The French word means exactly the same thing—"go with God," or "I commend you to God." Our English "goodbye" is also a shortened version of "God be with you," as is the Italian *addio*.

Q. "Of course, I know what A.M. and P.M. mean—before and after noon. But I really do not know what the words and initials stand for, and I'll bet a lot of other people are in the same boat."

A. I'm sure you're right. We take so much for granted. At least you have an inquiring mind. A.M. stands for *ante meridiem*. You may recall from the Prefixes chapter that *ante* is Latin for "before." P.M. stands for *post meridiem—post* "after" and *meridiem* "midday, noon." Simple.

Q. "Is *atom* a coined word?"

A. No. In medieval times, an atom was the smallest measure of time, 15/94 of a second. Atom is from the Greek *atemno,* meaning "not cut"—something so small it cannot be divided.

Q. "Which are the most beautiful words in the English language?"

A. Ian Warden, columnist of the Canberra (Australia) *Times*, recently conducted a poll. Warren's favorite lists of beautiful words were these:

Madrigal, crumhorn, heliotrope, desuetude, larkspur, baroque, lapwing, virago, lyre, persimmon.

Callow, ocean, epiphany, cedar, bluebell, grace, melody, cinnamon, sapphire, yesterday.

Calypso, carousel, dulcimer, hyacinth, icicle, lollipop, peccadillo, parasol, quince, sparkle.

Harlot, sumptuous, mushroom, cashmere, apricot, petal, moth, amber, lilith, mellifluous.

Elegant, silver, flute, celibate, salad, tinsel, limpid, slake, purple, trellis.

The ugly word lists, with Warden's comments in parentheses, were:

Artichoke, itchy, extrapolate, eschew, hemorrhoids, uncle, awkward, sausage, verb, and lugubrious. ("I think that 'hemorrhoids' is far too handsome for the list," commented Warden.)

Bunch, bug, greasy, guffaw, haggis, oboe, scabbard, scrounge, and weasel. ("I find the inclusion of oboe quite inexplicable.")

Another ugly-word list was sent in to the contest by the Reverend Peter Hassell Davis of "the bucolic hamlet of Yass," as follows:

Gargoyles, defalcate, dreck, excoriate, inspissate, macadamisation, meritocracy, mundungus, saxophone, scabrous, and stercoraceous.

Mr. Davis also submitted a list of beautiful words, and though they didn't win a prize, Warden thought it worth noting that it included allelomorph, declutition, and algorithm.

Jack Smith, the *Los Angeles Times* columnist, has chosen his ten most beautiful words as follows: parasol, larkspur, icicle, sparkle, cashmere, lapwing, silver, flute, apricot, and hyacinth.

Any list of the "most beautiful" or "most ugly" must, of course, be arbitrary. There's nothing and no one to stop you from making up your own. One of my favorites, for instance, is *serendipity*—as much for its up and down flow of syllables as for the fact that it sounds so much like its meaning—coming across wonderful finds by chance. According to the *Oxford English Dictionary*, the word was coined by Horace Walpole from the title of a fairy tale, "The Three Princes of Serendip." (Serendip or Serendib was an old name for Sri Lanka.) These three princes were, according to Walpole, "always making discoveries, by accidents and sagacity, of things they were not in quest of."

Dr. Wilfred Funk, author of many books on word origins, once made a list of what he considered the most beautiful words in the English language. These were his choices:

Tranquil, golden, hush, thrush, lullabye, chimes, murmuring, luminous, damask, cerulean, melody, marigold, jonquil, oriole, tendril, myrrh, mignonette, gossamer, fawn, dawn, chalice, anemone, alyssum, mist, oleander, amaryllis, rosemary, camellia, asphodel, halcyon.

Q. "Why do we use both *demi* and *semi* to indicate half?"
A. You forgot *hemi*! It also means half! The answer is that demi and semi came down to us from Latin and hemi from Greek. Thus we have semiquaver, which is a 16th note in music, demisemiquaver,

which is a 32nd note and my favorite of all, hemidemisemiquaver—
a half of a half of a half of a quaver, which is a 64th note.

Q. "I am Jewish, and I've always been curious about the derivation
of the derogatory term *kike*. Can you shed any light?"
A. According to H.L. Mencken in his book *The American Language*,
religious Jews who immigrated to America in the late 1800's and early
1900's—knowing no English and totally unaware of the customs of
the strange country in which they found themselves—were lustily
derided by their more experienced coreligionists as *kylechdiks*.

Once aware of this word's origin, some of the hostility attached
to the word is diffused. At about the same time, Italians were called
"wops"—not such a derogatory term when you learn its origin—*guappo*,
Italian dialect for "dandy."

Q. "When a person is asked to leave a bar, why do we say 'he's
86'd?' "
A. According to the *American Thesaurus of Slang*, it was a password
devised by soda fountain clerks meaning "we're all out of the item
ordered." This term wandered to bartenders and now means "don't
serve him any more" or "ask him to leave." The number code was
extensive, and included 99 for the fountain manager, 98 for assistant
manager, 33 for a cherry-flavored Coke, 55 for root beer, and 19 for
a banana split. Presumably, some of the young soda fountain clerks
grew up to be bartenders and took their code-numbers with them.

Q. "Is there one word in the English language which includes all the
vowels in the proper order?"
A. No—there are two! Facetious and abstemious are the ones. (Can
you think of any others?)

Q. "My dictionary—I don't know about yours—gives the plural of
fish as '*fish* or *fishes*.' And it stops right there. Then it goes on to
define the word, as one of the super-class Pisces. I am a science
supply house copywriter, and I'd like to know, 'What is the difference
between fish (plural) and fishes (plural).' I am having a confrontation
with several of my co-writers as to which is correct."

A. The answer, a rather abstract one, is still easy to understand. Fish, the plural, pertains to many fish of the same type. Lots of flounder, for example. But if you have a bucket of flounder, mackerel, halibut, and sole, then we would have fishes. The same differentiation applies to the word *people* (plural) vs. *peoples*. *People* means a homogeneous group, and peoples applies to a heterogeneous grouping (the people on the 17th floor; the peoples of Asia).

Q. "What can you tell me about one of my favorite words, which I try to slip into the conversation whenever I can—*gallimaufry*."
A. If you're slipping it into conversations, I guess you know it means "a hodge-podge, a stew." We got it from the French, and there's a theory that the French coined it from the words "galer," "to live a gay life," and "mafrer" which means "to eat voraciously."

Q. "Why do some people say '*God bless you,*' when a person sneezes?"
A. During the Middle Ages, people thought that when a person sneezed the soul left the person's body for a few seconds, and the devil, always on the lookout for human souls, could snatch it out of the air. To prevent this a good friend would quickly say, "God bless you," and the devil would be frightened off.

Q. "Why do we call a peanut a *goober*?"
A. That's an easy one. Goober came to us—as did the peanut—from Africa, and goober is just a variation of the Congolese word for "peanut," *nguba*.

One of my callers did ask about the word *gubernatorial*. I answered that since President Carter had been a peanut farmer, the word originated from peanuts. Of course, this was just my phenomenally phrenetic wit at work. Gubernatorial really derives from the Latin *gubernator*, meaning "governor."

Q. "What's a *googol*? It sounds like baby-talk."
A. A googol is the name for the number 1 followed by 100 zeroes, and it's an important mathematical term used and accepted by math-

ematicians throughout the world. It was coined half-humorously by the young nephew of an important American mathematician, Edward Kasner. (A googolplex is the figure 1 followed by an *infinite* number of zeroes.)

Q. " 'The Greeks had a word for it' is a common expression, and I've always wondered what the word was."
A. The phrase was the title of a 1929 play by Zoe Akins. The word was *hetaerae*, a high-class courtesan. The hetaerae (pronounced hih-TIR-ee) were akin to Japanese geisha girls—women trained to provide conversation and entertainment for a price.

Q. "What's wrong with using 'hopefully' when you're talking about something you hope will happen, and why are wordsmiths and grammarians so dead set against it?"
A. I cannot answer your question more clearly than to quote Philip Howard, in *New Words for Old*.

"Clarity must be the principal criterion in any linguistic question. Hopefully should therefore be disqualified because it is ambiguous and obscure, as well as illiterate and ugly." Mr. Howard cites this sentence: "England will bat hopefully after lunch" as a statement that admits of two grammatical constructions, each yielding a different meaning. It could mean, according to the old sense of hopefully, that the English batsmen (and their supporters) will be full of hope; which might be a triumph of hope over experience. It could also mean that it is hoped that the rain will stop, or the other side will declare, or England will dismiss their opponents' tail-enders, so that they can start batting after lunch. There is nothing wrong with 'it is hoped' and much right with it." Mr. Howard also states: "The aberrant modern use of 'hopefully' seems to have been widely introduced in the 1950s by sloppy American academics." *Hopefully* is "a pompous euphemism for the plainer verb: I, we, or they hope, or it is hoped."

I feel that it is confusing to have the same word doing duty for two different meanings: "in a hopeful fashion" and "it is to be hoped." But so many people use hopefully in the second sense that it is my guess it will be generally accepted as proper in years to come.

Q. "Why is *I* always capitalized. Is it a question of ego?"
A. *I* is capitalized because when manuscripts were copied by hand a small i could so easily get lost or become attached to the letter preceding or following it. To differentiate *I* as a separate word, copyists began to capitalize it.

Q. "What about that good old footnote word, *ibid?*"
A. It's short for *ibidem*, which literally translated means "in the same place," and it's used in footnotes and bibliographies to refer to the book, chapter, article, or page cited just before.

Another very common Latin abbreviation is *op. cit. (opere citate)*. It means "in the work referred to."

Q. "Whence cometh *maitre d'*? I know that *maitre* means 'master' and *d'* means 'of.' But master of what?"
A. Don't castigate yourself. It's short for maitre d'hotel—meaning a head steward or butler. If you asked ten people on the street, I'm not sure one would know the answer. Curiosity is the first step towards knowledge.

Q. "I am always seeking to avoid *obfuscation,* but it occurs to me that I really don't understand the derivation of the word, although I know it means to obscure."
A. It comes from the Latin *ob*, a prefix that makes a verb more intense, and *fuscare*, "to darken." When it becomes dark, things do become obscure. The *American Heritage Dictionary* gives the primary meaning of this word as "to render indistinct or dim; darken: *The fog obfuscated the shore*." Secondary meaning is to "to confuse or becloud."

In his book *A Pleasure in Words* (Simon and Schuster, 1981), Eugene Maleska gives a wonderful example of obfuscation. See if you can translate it before you read its real meaning:

"It was Joseph Smyth's quotidian routine to ruminate peripatetically in the course of his peregrination to the urban educational establishment where he served as a custodial engineer. Every morning, a frowzy mendicant importuned him. Preoccupied with cosmotellurian cognitions, Smythe would altruistically deposit currency in the schnorrer's stannic container."

Here's the translation!

"It was Joe Smyth's daily routine to ponder while walking on his journey to the city school where he served as a janitor. Every morning a shabby beggar would approach him abruptly and ask for a handout. Lost in thoughts about heaven and earth, Smith would unselfishly drop some coins into the beggar's tin cup."

I think these two paragraphs take the cake!**

Q. "I have a great fear of spiders. Is there a word to describe my *phobia*?"
A. There certainly is: arachnophobia. There's a word to describe just about every kind of fear. Here are some others.

acero—sourness	antlo—flood
acro—pinnacles	apeiro—infinity
agora—open places	api—bees
aichuro—points	astheno—weakness
ailouro—cats	ata—ruin
akoustico—sound	atelo—imperfection
algo—pain	aulo—flute
alto—height	aurora—auroral lights
amatho—dust	bacillo—microbes
andro—man	baro—gravity
angino—narrowness	batho—depth
Anglo—England	bato—walking
anthropo—human beings	balone—needles

**According to the *Morris Dictionary of Word and Phrase Origins*, a form of entertainment among blacks in the South in former years was a contest to determine the most graceful pair of walkers. Couples would walk in a circle around a cake, which was the prize, and the winners would "take the cake." From such contests evolved the *cakewalk*, a popular kind of strutting dance. The custom of using a cake as a contest prize goes back to the Greeks when the man who could stick with his drinking longest "took the cake." In Ireland, dancing contests were held in which a cake was the prize.

batracho—reptiles
biblio—books
bronto—thunder
carcino—cancer
cardio—heart condition
chaeto—hair
cheimato—cold
ciono—snow
chrometo—money
chromo—color
chronol—duration
clino—going to bed
cnido—stings
copro—feces
cryo—ice, frost
crystallo—crystals
cymo—sea swells
cyno—dogs
demo—crowds
demono—demons
dendro—trees
dike—justice
dora—fur
eispotro—mirrors
elektro—electricity
eleuthero—freedom
enete—pins
entomo—insects
eoso—dawn
eremito—solitude
ergo—word
erythro—blushing
Gallo—France
gameto—marriage
geno—set
Germano—Germany
grapho—writing
gymno—nudity
gyno—women

hapto—touch
harpato—robbers
hedono—pleasure
hippo—horses
homichlo—fog
horme—shock
hygro—dampness
hypegia—responsibility
hypno—sleep
hypso—height
ideo—ideas
kahorraphia—failure
keno—void
ketagelo—ridicule
kineto—motion
koni—dust
kypho—stooping
lalo—speech
limno—string
linono—lakes
logo—word
lysso—insanity
mania—insanity
mastigo—flogging
mechano—machinery
metallo—metals
meteoro—meteors
mono—one thing
musico—music
muso—mice
necro—corpses
negro—blacks
nelo—glass
neo—new things
nepho—clouds
noso—disease
ocho—vehicles
odonto—teeth
oilo—home

olfacto—smell
ommeta—eyes
oneiro—dreams
ophio—snakes
ornitho—birds
ourano—heaven
pan—everything
partheno—young girls
patroio—heredity
peccato—sinning
pediculo—lice
penia—poverty
phago—swallowing
plasmo—ghost
pharmaco—drugs
phono—speaking aloud
pnigero—smothering
poine—punishment
poly—many things
poto—drink
pterono—feather
Russo—Russia
rypo—soiling
scio—shadows

sela—flashes
sidero—stars
sino—China
sito—food
spermo—germs
staso—standing
stygio—hell
syphilo—syphilis
tacho—speed
terato—monsters
terdeka—number 13
thaaso—sitting idle
thalasso—sea
thanato—death
theo—god
thermo—heat
thixo—touching
toco—childbirth
toxi—poison
traumato—wounds
tremo—trembling
typano—inoculations
zelo—jealousy

An interesting addendum to the root "hedano" is the suggestion made by one of my callers that the original title of Woody Allen's film *Annie Hall* was *Ann Hedonia*, meaning the inability to feel pleasure.

If you like any of the above categories; just add—*phile* to it instead of—phobe. Someone who's very fond of spiders would be an arachnophile.

Q. "A close friend exclaimed loudly at seeing two donkeys meandering down the road, 'Look at that pace of asses.' Was he correct? Can you add anything to my fledgling collection of unusual collective nouns, such as a 'gaggle of geese?' "

A. Yes, he was correct. And here's a myriad of others.

A pure of meadowlarks
Gam or pod of whales
Pod of walrus
Trip of seal
Bag of birds
Hand of bananas
Bevy or covey of quail
Pride of lions
Spring of teal
Ascension or exaltation of larks
Charm of goldfinch
Nide of pheasant
Plump of duck
Watch of nightingales
Yard of moose
Muster of peacocks
Swarm or yeast of bees
Colony of ants
Sord of mallards
Cete of badgers
Drift of hogs
Kindle of kittens

Shrewdness of apes
Skin of wildfowl
Skulk of vermin
Covert of coots
Wisp of snipe
Gang of buffaloes and/or elk
Sloth of bears
Sounder of wild hog
Clowder of wildcats
Barren of mules
Stud of mares
Rag of colts
Sedge of herons
Murmuration of starlings
Fall of woodcocks
Smack of jellyfish
Hover of trout
Siege of herons
Host of sparrows
Sounder of swine
Business of ferrets

Q. "Here's a stumper. Why do we use the abbreviation *lb.* for pound?"
A. It's curious, isn't it? And I'm glad you inquired. Lb. comes from libra—the Latin word for pound. It appears to have originated during the Renaissance in manuscript writing.

Q. "From where do we derive the name *quack* for a lousy doctor?"
A. It is short for "quacksalver"—from the early modern Dutch *quasalvern*, which meant "to cure with home remedies." It's easy to see how this came to mean "an untrained person who pretends to have medical knowledge," thus, our modern nutty "doctor."

Q. "Someone told me that Red Square in Moscow had the same name under the czars. Is this true?"
A. In Russia, the word *krasnya* ("Red") doesn't necessarily mean something revolutionary at all. It has long been used as a synonym

for "beautiful." Red Square was always called that as the biggest and most impressive square in the city.

Q. "Why is the *ye* in ye Old Curiosity Shop pronounced like the?"
A. English originally had a letter called *thorn* which expressed the "th" sound. The thorn looked very much like our present-day Y, and printers began to substitute a Y for the thorn—giving us YE. But as you noted, it is pronounced the. Thorn got its name because the Anglo-Saxons used words which began with or stressed certain letters to name those letters.

For Further Reading

There are two indispensable tools for the student of language. One is a library card, and the other is a dictionary. There are many dictionaries, abridged, unabridged, and specialized. Here are just a few worth exploring.

UNABRIDGED DICTIONARIES

Oxford English Dictionary (OED), 10 vols. Oxford: Oxford University Press

Random House Compact Unabridged Dictionary. New York: Random House, 1995

Random House Dictionary of the English Language. New York: Random House, 1966.

Webster's New Twentieth Century Dictionary. 2nd Edition. New York: Simon & Schuster, 1983.

ABRIDGED DICTIONARIES

The American Heritage Dictionary of the English Language. Boston: Houghton Mifflin.

Funk & Wagnall's Standard College Dictionary. New York: Funk & Wagnall, 1997.

Macmillan Contemporary Dictionary. New York: Macmillan, 1979.

The Random House College Dictionary. Rev. Ed. New York: Random House, 1980.

Webster's New Collegiate Dictionary. Springfield, Mass.: Merriam-Webster, 1981.

Webster's New World Dictionary of the English Language. 2nd College Ed. New York: Simon & Schuster, 1980.

SPECIALIZED DICTIONARIES

American Slang. New York: Harper & Row, 1993.

Brewer's Dictionary of Phrase and Fable. New York: Harper & Row, 1981.

Columbia Dictionary of Modern European Literature. New York: Columbia University Press, 1980.

Encyclopedia of American Family Names. New York: HarperCollins, 1996.

Illustrated Reverse Dictionary. Reader's Digest Press, 1990.

New York Public Library Desk Reference. Englewood Cliffs, NJ: Prentice-Hall, 1995

Merriam-Webster's Medical Desk Dictionary. Springfield, Mass.: Merriam-Webster, 1993.

Merriam-Webster's Rhyming Dictionary. Springfield, Mass.: Merriam-Webster, 1991.

Oxford Dictionary of Quotations and Thesaurus. Oxford: Oxford University Press, 1996

Ultimate Visual Dictionary. DK Publishing, 1994.

BIOGRAPHICAL DICTIONARIES

Dictionary of National Biography. London: Oxford: Oxford University Press, 1921-present.

Merriam-Webster's Biographical Dictionary. Springfield, Mass.: Merriam-Webster, 1995.

SYNONYMS AND ANTONYMS

Bartlett's Roget's Thesaurus. Boston: Little Brown, 1995.

Roget's Thesaurus in Dictionary Form. New York: Putnam, 1978.

Synonym Finder. Emmaus, Pa.: Rodale Press, 1978.

STYLE MANUALS

Chicago Manual of Style. Chicago: University of Chicago Press.

Columbia Guide to Standard American English. New York: Columbia University Press, 1995.

The Careful Writer. Bernstein. New York: Atheneum Press, 1994.

Elements of Style. Strunk & White. New York: Macmillan, 1979.

VOCABULARY, WRITER AIDS

Aspects of Language. William J. Entwistle. New York: Macmillan, 1954.

Essential Software for Writers. Bender. Writer's Digest, 1996.

An Exaltation of Larks: or, The Venereal Game. New York: Viking Press, 1968.

The Joys of Yiddish. Leo Rosten. New York: McGraw-Hill, 1968.

Language in Thought and Action. S.I. Hayakawa, with Arther A. Berger and Arthur Chandler. New York: Harcourt Brace Jovanovich, 1978.

The Mother Tongue. Lancelot Hogben. London: Secker and Warburg.

New Words for Old. Philip Howard. New York: Oxford University Press, 1977.

A Pleasure in Words. Eugene T. Maleska. New York: Simon & Schuster, 1982.

Strictly Speaking: Will America Be the Death of English? Edwin Newman. New York: Bobbs-Merrill, 1975.

Words and Things. Roger Williams Brown. New York: Free Press, 1968.

Writer's Guide to Book Editors, Publishers, and Literary Agents. Prima Press, 1997.

Writing for Money. Oberlin. Writer's Digest, 1994.

SPELLING AIDS

Bad Speller's Dictionary. Krensky and Linfield. 1995.

The Portable Handbook: An Index to Grammar, Usage and the Research Paper. William Herman. New York: Holt, Rinehart & Winston, 1978.

Prentice-Hall Handbook for Writers. Leggett, Mead, and Charvat. Englewood Cliffs, NJ: 1982.

Webster's New World Speller-Divider: The 33,000 Most-Used Words Spelled and Syllabified. New York: William Collins, 1971.

Index

ALSO AVAILABLE FROM BANDANNA BOOKS

Don't Panic: The Procrastinator's Guide to Writing an Effective Term Paper. Steven Posusta. Clearly written, Posusta's method has helped hundreds of freshmen and sophomores avoid a nightmare of anxiety. 64pp. ISBN 0-942208-42-0. $9.95

First Person Intense: A Prose Anthology. Edited and with introduction by Sasha Newborn. Twenty-five first-person prose stylists including Charles Bukowski, Fielding Dawson, Richard Currey, Richard Kostelanetz, Rochelle Holt Dubois. 1978. With photos and bios. 188pp. ISBN 0-930012-14-3. $10.00

Sappho: The Poems. Translation by Sasha Newborn. Greece's greatest lyric poet. 47pp., Revised Edition, 2nd Printing. ISBN 0-942208-11-0. $5.00

Surfing: A Royal Sport. Jack London's discover and description of the new sport of surf-riding on long boards in Hawaii in 1911, a chapter from *The Cruise of the Snark.* ISBN 0-924208-12-9. 18pp. $2.00

Benigna Machiavelli. Charlotte Perkins Gilman. 1916. Unusual semi-autobiographical novel of young adulthood by feminist and utopian writer Gilman. ISBN 0-942208-18-8. 179pp. $10.00

Original 1855 Leaves of Grass. Walt Whitman. Humanist editing by A.S. Ash and reset from the original 1855 edition. 117pp., Second printing. ISBN 0-9422208-08-0. $8.00

A Backward Glance over Traveled Roads. Walt Whitman. The 1888 account of writing Leaves of Grass. 20pp. ISBN 0-942208-41-2. $2.00

Italian for Opera Lovers. Edited by Hassan W. Ebron. Italian opera terms defined. ISBN 0-942208-17-X. 39pp. $3.50

Areopagitica: Freedom of the Press. John Milton. Humanist editing by A.S. Ash. Survey of censorship ancient and modern. 44pp. Third Printing. ISBN 0-942208-04-8 $5.00

The Apology of Socrates, & The Crito. Plato. Socrates' defense in the trial for his life and his refusal to escape. Humanist editing by A.S. Ash. 46pp., Third Printing. ISBN 0-942208-05-6 $5.00

Ordering information: Bandanna Books, 319-B Anacapa St., Santa Barbara CA 93101. (805) 962-9915. FAX (805) 564-3566. Email: bandanna@west.net. Website for credit card sales: http://www.west.net/~bandanna. Please include $2 for shipping and handling.